Thanksgiving Joy

A Cornucopia of Stories, Songs, Poems, Recipes, and Traditions

Tranquility Press
2016

Thanksgiving Joy: A Cornucopia of Stories, Songs, Poems, Recipes, and Traditions

Edited by Faith Lynn

Tranquility Press
1102 S. Austin Ave. #110-234
Georgetown TX 78626
www.TranquilityPress.net

ISBN 978-0990497790

For
Faith and April
with love

In memory of my grandmothers,
Lorene Koch Liesmann
and Lillian Schmidt Walker,
and my mother-in-law, Mary Hardister Lynn,
all of whom shared a love for
the gathering of family at Thanksgiving
that I inherited

Contents

A Note from the Author

"Bring the recipe for that pie your mom always made that I loved so much."

"Please give us some more of that Sunshine Relish for Christmas. And if you have plenty, give us some extra jars of it, because our friends want some, too!"

"I thought I loved apple pie, but when I have it anywhere but Mimi's, I'm disappointed."

"Cantaloupe pie? I don't think I want to try it, thanks anyway...Wow, that's *good*! Can I have a bigger piece?"

"How do you always get your venison so tender?"

"And the blue ribbon goes to..."

Comments like those were the genesis of this book. My husband and I both have well-loved recipes that have been passed down for generations. It's now time to pass them on to the next generation. As I went through the ones I wanted to share first, Thanksgiving kept coming to mind. That's not surprising, since food is such a major part of that holiday. I thought it would be helpful to include some ideas for hosting a big, traditional, family Thanksgiving, since the time is fast approaching when the next generation will take over that responsibility.

The idea for the book was further cemented by a comment made at a Thanksgiving a couple of years ago. I had hosted the family along with our neighbors and some friends. As they were leaving, one of them said, "This was what Thanksgiving is supposed to be. I really liked the readings and the music and everything. We usually just eat, and that's all the day is about. It's good to remember that we're supposed to be giving thanks. We're all so blessed, just to be alive, and in this time and place; and we don't appreciate it like we should."

I agree with that sentiment, and wanted to make note of some of the things we'd enjoyed that day to remember. This led to the playlist and the collection of poems and other readings included. By the time I finished, I realized the book was meant to be shared with a wider audience. And while there are thousands more ideas than one book has room for, some of these tips and suggestions may prove helpful to you. At the least, perhaps they can inspire your own vision of what Thanksgiving should be.

Even so, the main purpose was to share a few family recipes and memories with the next generation; so throughout the book, you will see a few comments directed to them, such as when I mention that a particular bowl was always used for Granny's fruit salad. Also, some recipes are written the old-fashioned way, with the ingredients given within the instructions instead of listed first, because that's the way they've been passed down.

Thanksgiving is one of the most-loved holidays in America, but it can be intimidating to host for the first time; and even after becoming comfortable with the routine, many people want a few new ideas to enliven the day. Whether you are a first-time host, will be on your own for the holiday, or are simply looking for a few fresh ideas to enhance an already-traditional celebration, I hope the tips, ideas, recipes, readings, and activities in this book help you find true Thanksgiving joy.

America's Holiday

Ask any American about the first Thanksgiving and you'll likely hear a story about hungry Pilgrims and "Indians" coming to save the day. There is some truth to that story, but there's also much more to the history of what has been called our national holiday.

No one knows the date or circumstances of the first time someone had the idea for a whole community to dedicate an entire day to giving thanks for their blessings. There were undoubtedly many such times in different cultures throughout human history; after all, harvest festivals celebrating plenty and appeasing the gods were celebrated as far back as ancient Mesopotamia. These usually included some sort of offering from the harvest to thank the gods, and at the same time remind these deities that their people needed favorable conditions for another good harvest the following year. In addition to the harvest sacrifices, songs and dancing, stories, and feasting were generally enjoyed as part of the seasonal dedications.

In ancient times, Greeks, Romans, and Egyptians each had a yearly harvest festival in which they thanked their respective gods for the harvest, and all celebrated with religious rituals, music, games, and feasting. Celts celebrated the harvest in the same way during their festival of Lughnasadh. Indigenous peoples the world over have created celebrations of gratefulness for harvests. Most tribes had a culture of thankfulness that was expressed throughout the year. The Jewish people have held a yearly harvest celebration known as Sukkot for thousands of years, and early Christians had several days of either feasting or fasting set aside each year for thanksgiving to God.

When Europeans began coming to the New World they brought these customs with them. Days of thanksgiving have been held in the Americas by people of European decent since at least the 1500s. These observances were sometimes spontaneous events to mark safe passage upon arrival in a new place or other such milestones. Other times they were held in accordance with a minor Catholic holiday, as was the case on May 29, 1541 in Texas' Palo Duro Canyon.

Francisco Vasquez de Coronado was on his famed search for gold in the fabled Seven Cities of Cibola when he and his army came in conflict with native tribes along the Rio Grande River outside what is now Albuquerque. He was told that if he and his men would leave, the tribe would give him a slave who they said was from Quivera, a City of Gold, as a guide.

The guide, whom Coronado called Turk, led the army of 1500 south for several months, eventually coming to Palo Duro Canyon, south of present-day Amarillo. Their first night in the canyon, a hailstorm hit, stampeding their horses, destroying equipment, ruining food, and spilling their water. Coronado sent out hunters, but they got lost. Luckily for them, a hospitable tribe of Teyas (a group of Apache) came to their aid, giving them food and supplies.

The Teyas also informed Coronado that he was heading the wrong direction; Quivera (which was a poor town without any gold) was far to the north. Turk had been purposely leading the Spaniards away from his people, trying to get them lost in the canyon. This deceit cost him his life.

With the assistance of the Teyas, Coronado readied to set out for Quivera on May 29, 1541, which happened to be the minor Catholic holiday Feast of the Ascension. Father Fray Juan De Padilla conducted a Mass to mark the Feast, and an actual feast followed. Reports of the event indicate that the Mass was witnessed by the natives, who watched the ritual in amazement, and later partook of the feast. There is no indication that the thanks given that day included appreciation for the help of the Teyas, although that would have been appropriate, since Coronado and his men would certainly have perished without it. Because this event was held on an already-established holiday, as were many of the other early observances, none of them were ever recognized as a momentous event worthy of commemorating.

It was different in Plymouth Plantation in 1621. It wasn't the fact of the Puritans' (often called Pilgrims) rejoicing in a good harvest that was different. An annual celebration of this type, called a "Harvest Home," had been observed by them for years. They also routinely had days of thanksgiving, although those days were spent in prayer, not in festival.

Nor was the Wampanoag's revelry unusual. The Wampanoag were a tribe of the Iroquois that lived in the area the Puritans settled. They observed a time of thankfulness seven times throughout the year. The festival at the end of harvest was a four-day celebration known as Da-yo-nun'-neo-quä na De-o-ha'-ko. The name means "Thanksgiving to Our Supporters." The "supporters" referred to are the "three sisters" of corn, beans, and squash, which served as the chief source of food for the Iroquois. They marked these occasions in much the same way as the English Harvest Home celebrations: with community gatherings, song and dance, games, prayers of thanksgiving, and, of course, feasting.

The 1621 event in Plymouth was the first (known) time the European culture and the American Indian culture combined into a single celebration. It is worth noting how and why this came about, because although the two groups had signed a treaty agreeing not to harass one another, each still viewed the other with suspicion.

The indigenous peoples already had experience with Europeans, with tragic results. The previous decimation of entire villages by white men made them wary. They were not helping the newcomers out of naivety, or because they especially liked or respected them. On the contrary, there was much they did not appreciate about these interlopers who stole their corn and treated the earth as disposable, personal property. However, the culture of the Wampanoag was that everyone worked together for the good of all; that one should help others when possible; and to be hospitable to guests even if they were unwelcome. They lived by this code, and so when the Puritans were suffering and helpless, the Wampanoag came to their aid. The native peoples didn't want the white men there, but, being true to their values, were resigned to make the best of the situation.

The Puritans were also living true to their values. They hadn't come to the New World to escape religious persecution so much as to find a place they could establish the "rule of saints," a new, "pure," Christian government. They believed they had been chosen by Jehovah (the name of God used by the Puritans) to form this government, and that doing so would bring the Messiah. Seeing themselves as God's agents, any interference with their plans was deemed to originate from Satan himself. The native population could be part of their one true, pure church if they accepted this rule; otherwise, they were an enemy of God to be overcome. This idea of Manifest Destiny was so deeply ingrained in their belief system that it was perpetuated for generations, and still has repercussions to this day: American exceptionalism and the belief that America was providentially founded as a Christian nation are continuations of the Manifest Destiny mindset.

How did two groups with such mutual distrust come together for a celebration? It began with the landing of the Mayflower in December of 1620. The journey from England had taken longer than expected, with two dire results: the foodstuffs the settlers brought with them were depleted, and it was too late to plant any crops, much less reap a harvest. Moreover, they were in an unfamiliar place and didn't know which plants were edible and which might be toxic.

They were also unprepared for the harshness of the weather. Although that winter was comparatively mild, the weeks after the Mayflower landed were stormy and freezing. The settlers had no permanent shelters yet, and illness was rampant. At times there were only six or seven healthy individuals in the entire settlement to care for the rest. Many died; of the 102 people who came ashore in December, by the spring of 1621, only 53 remained alive.

In March, while sowing the seeds they had brought from their homeland, the settlers were surprised by a native man who walked up, said "Welcome!" in English, and asked for a beer! His name was Samoset, from the Pemaquid tribe. He had learned some English when he had been taken as a slave by European fishermen some years before. Samoset had a friend, Tisquantum, who spoke even better English. Tisquantum (whom the settlers called Squanto) had also been taken to Europe as a slave. Both of these men had eventually found their way back to their homeland. Despite the hardships they'd suffered at the hands of white men, they befriended the newcomers. Tisquantum was especially helpful.

Be thankful in all circumstances, for this is God's will for you. ~1 Thessalonians 5:18

In fact, had it not been for him, the remaining 53 settlers would undoubtedly have died within the year. He not only gave them corn to plant, he showed them how to plant it so that it would grow. That corn became the Puritans' staple food, as their own seeds did not do well in American soil and produced very little food. He showed them the plants that were safe to eat, or that could be used as medicines, and which to avoid. He taught them the best ways to catch fish, and how to build lodging with materials from the area. He taught them to survive in a world very new and different from the one they had left. He also arranged a meeting between the Wampanoag chief Massasoit and the settlers, and brokered a peace treaty.

Thanks to Tisquantum, by the end of that summer, Plymouth Plantation had built seven homes for its settlers and four community buildings. They brought in good crops of "Indian corn" and had learned how to harvest all manner of fish and shellfish. They were so happy with their situation that the Governor of the plantation called for a special time of rejoicing and festivity in September, 1621. This festival has come to be known as the First Thanksgiving. Primary sources state that the Puritans enjoyed various entertainments, including "exercising arms" (as in target practice and shooting contests), and say there were "many of the Indians coming amongst" them.

Some historians believe that since the Wampanoag had helped produce the bounty, they were invited by the settlers to help celebrate it. Others believe the Wampanoag were brought to the settlement by the noise of the guns, thinking it was being attacked. This would be in accord with their treaty, which stated that if either group was attacked, the other would come to their aid. There is no evidence either way, although the account seems to read more like the native people arrived unexpectedly.

However they came to be there, it was the time of the final harvest celebration for the Wampanoag, and the Puritans were having a Harvest Home, so they did fellowship together for three days. The bounty of the crops and gardens were shared; men of the settlement had gone "fowling" and brought in many birds; the Wampanoag brought in five deer. Together they feasted and celebrated. This was a purely secular celebration, at least as far as the Puritans were concerned.

It wasn't all play, though; business was taken care of, too. Whether by planning or happenstance, since they were all together, another treaty was made. This one stated that the Wampanoag would subject themselves to King James. They did this so that they would have the protection of the king's men. Another tribe, a group of Algonquian which was larger and more powerful, was threatening the Wampanoag. The guns and cannons of the settlers would help even the odds. Interestingly, the treaty did not state that King James or his men would give any type of aid to the Wampanoag, even though that was the verbal agreement. In fact, the settlers had purposely established their settlement outside of the King's charter area (so they could set up their own government), and they had no right to speak for him.

A three-day harvest celebration shared by natives and new settlers was unusual, but it was not considered something to commemorate for another two centuries. Before that happened, other thanksgivings were held.

The first official declaration of a day of thanksgiving in America was two years after that first harvest celebration. Two months of great heat and drought in the summer of 1623 made the Puritans anxious about their crops. Despite the prayers of the individuals, the corn withered away and the beans were scorched, with no prospect of rain in sight. Thus the authorities called for a day of public fasting and prayer.

The group assembled in the church and prayed together for over 8 hours. Although it was clear and hot when they gathered in the morning, by that evening clouds were appearing, and the next day a gentle rain came. Two weeks of showers revived the crops, and that fall the plantations' harvest was bountiful. Feeling that it would be ungrateful to give thanks in private for something which could be obtained only by public prayer, a day was appointed to openly give praise and thanksgiving to God.

This is the day that the Puritans themselves would have considered the first Thanksgiving. To them, a holiday was really a holy day, spent solemnly in prayer as a group. A similar event occurred in Massachusetts Bay Colony in 1631. Settlers were running low on supplies, and feared the relief ship had been lost at sea. It arrived safely, and the following day was spent in thanks to God in prayer.

Plymouth Colony proclaimed its first Thanksgiving in gratitude for general blessings of the year in November, 1668. The Court asked all the congregations in the Colony to devote a day of thanksgiving for "the goodnes of God to us in the continuance of our civill and religious liberties, the generall health that wee have enjoyed, and that it hath pleased God in some comfortable measure to blesse us in the fruites of the earth. [sic]"

A few years later, in 1676, Edward Rawson, clerk for Charlestown, Massachusetts, was directed by the council of that town to proclaim June 29 of that year as a Day of Thanksgiving (see the Proclamation in the Readings). The reason for this was that the town had been spared desolation during the atrocity which came to be known as King Philip's War. The entire township was instructed to spend the day standing before God in thanksgiving for this fact. Even this day was a limited event, held by one township.

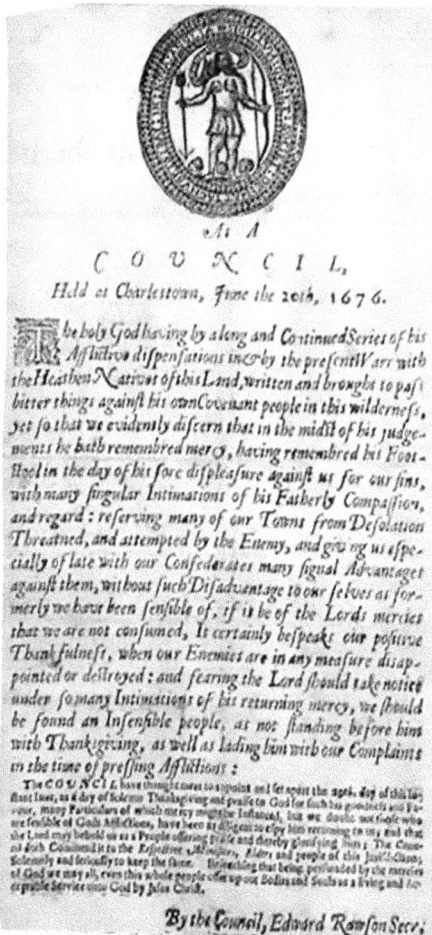

The first official national Day of Thanksgiving occurred on December 18, 1777. The Continental Congress proclaimed the day the previous November, to acknowledge the hand of Providence in the successful outcome of the Revolution and, at the same time, beseech the Lord for further blessings in the labors of the citizens, the crops of the field, and the establishment of schools and churches, all of which they recognized as essential for independence and peace. Work and play alike were discouraged on the day set aside for prayer.

There were a few more national days of Thanksgiving designated in the next decades, but the observation of the holiday fell aside on the national level after 1815. Various states kept the practice, however, so it remained in the minds of some citizens. One of these was Sarah Josepha Hale.

A young lady from New Hampshire, Hale turned to writing and editing to make a living after her husband died. Having grown up with a yearly New England Thanksgiving, she felt the nation should unite in this endeavor, and many of her writings included heartwarming scenes of the celebration, like this one from her 1827 novel *Northwood*:

> The table...was now intended for the whole household, every child having a seat on this occasion; and the more the better, it being considered an honor for a man to sit down to his Thanksgiving dinner surrounded by a large family. The provision is always sufficient for a multitude, every farmer in the country being, at this season of the year, plentifully supplied, and every one proud of displaying his abundance and prosperity.
>
> The roasted turkey took precedence on this occasion, being placed at the head of the table; and well did it become its lordly station, sending forth the rich odor of its savory stuffing, and finely covered with the froth of the basting...the celebrated pumpkin pie, an indispensable part of a good and true Yankee Thanksgiving; the

size of the pie usually denoting the gratitude of the party who prepares the feast… Plates of pickles, preserves and butter, and all the necessaries for increasing the seasoning of the viands to the demand of each palate, filled the interstices on the table, leaving hardly sufficient room for the plates of the company, a wine glass and two tumblers for each, with a slice of wheat bread lying on one of the inverted tumblers…

There was a huge plum pudding, custards and pies of every name and description ever known in Yankee land; yet the pumpkin pie occupied the most distinguished niche. There were also several kinds of rich cake, and a variety of sweetmeats and fruits. On the sideboard was ranged a goodly number of decanters and bottles; the former filled with currant wine, and the latter with excellent cider and ginger beer…

Hale used her platform as writer and editor at some the country's most widely-read ladies' magazines to continually bring the idea of Thanksgiving before her readers for decades. Beginning in the 1840s, she encouraged all governors to proclaim the holiday in their state, and urged Congress to adopt the day nationally.

Hale later explained why she felt a national day of Thanksgiving was important. "…an appropriate tribute of gratitude to God to set apart one day of Thanksgiving in each year; and autumn is the time when the overflowing garners of America call for this expression of joyful gratitude," she wrote; and, "There is a deep moral influence in these periodical seasons of rejoicing, in which a whole community participate. They bring out, and together, as it were, the best sympathies of our nature…"

In addition to the religious aspects, Hale saw the possibilities of such a holiday in fostering a feeling of unity across the nation. As she wrote in 1860, "Everything that contributes to bind us in one vast empire together, to quicken the sympathy that makes us feel from the icy North to the sunny South that we are one family, each a member of a great and free Nation, not merely the unit of a remote locality, is worthy of being cherished. We have sought to reawaken and increase this sympathy, believing that the fine filaments of the affections are stronger than laws to keep the Union of our States sacred in the hearts of our people… We believe our Thanksgiving Day, if fixed and perpetuated, will be a great and sanctifying promoter of this national spirit."

This was an especially persuasive argument as the country became divided by the Civil War. Her plea was not heeded at that time, but Hale did not give up; three years later she wrote to President Lincoln, again bringing forth the idea. We don't know whether Lincoln ever received her letter (she sent it to his Secretary, whom she knew personally, asking him to forward or speak on her behalf) or, if he did, whether it influenced him, but in the fall of 1863, Lincoln did issue such a proclamation. He did so again in 1864, and every year since then has seen a Presidential Proclamation of Thanksgiving Day in the U.S.

Gratitude is not only the greatest of virtues, but the parent of all others. ~Marcus Tullius Cicero

THANKSGIVING Menu

Entree' of Health, Wealth & Happiness, Garnished with True Love, Generosity & Contentment

The Feast

For many people, the dinner is the highlight of Thanksgiving; but there are a few things to consider before that. Following are some tips and recipes to help the Thanksgiving meal become the feast you desire.

- Have breakfast planned the day before.

Depending on what time the big feast will be, you may choose to have a large or small breakfast; but you will want your kitchen free and clean to make the dinner, so allow plenty of time to prepare, eat, and clean up after breakfast. Add a little extra time to relax, too; you don't want to spend all day in the kitchen.

- Write out your menu and make sure you'll have plenty of pots and pans to cook everything.

Determine whether you'll need to make one or more dishes in a slow cooker, or if you'll ask anyone else to contribute to the meal. Will you need to purchase or borrow a separate burner or a large pot?

- Write out your guest list and make sure you can serve everyone.

Do you have plenty of plates, bowls, flatware, glasses, and napkins? Will you need to borrow an extra table? Do you need a tablecloth? Plan seating for everyone. You don't have to assign seating (although you can if you want to) but be sure there's a place for everyone to sit down and enjoy the meal. Purchase or borrow any needed items.

- Review all recipes ahead of time.

Shop in advance to ensure you have all the necessary ingredients before stores run short. This is also the time to plan how long to allow for the preparation of various dishes. See the timeline at the end of this chapter for help planning.

• Think about how you'll serve dinner.

Will it be buffet style, or will you set the table? Decide ahead of time which serving dish you will use for each entrée. If you have bakeware that you can also serve from, you'll save time setting the table, and the food will stay warmer longer. Make sure you have proper serving spoons, ladles, and a carving knife and fork if the turkey will be carved at the table. Don't forget condiments. If you don't have a butter dish or gravy boat, how will you serve these items? If you plan how to serve every dish ahead of time, it will save headaches later.

• Most people wish to begin the meal with a prayer or declaration of thanks, and/or a toast.

People won't enjoy the feast if it's cold, so you may want to limit the number of speakers before dinner. During the meal or at the end works just as well for any remaining blessings, speeches, or toasts.

> TIP: If you don'thave a gravy boat, use a coffeepot for the gravy. Don't run the gravy through the coffeemaker, of course; just put it in a coffeepot, and turn on the heating plate of the coffemaker to keep it warm. Give it an occasionaly shake or stir so it doesn't stick or get too thick. It's easy to pour the gravy from the coffeepot at the table. Lacking both gravy boat and coffeemaker, a thermos may also be used.

GRAINS OF PARCHED CORN

Thanksgiving dinner was good. Pa had shot a wild goose for it. Ma had to stew the goose because there was no fireplace, and no oven in the little stove. But she made dumplings in the gravy. There were corn dodgers and mashed potatoes. There were butter, and milk, and stewed dried plums. And three grains of parched corn lay beside each tin plate.

At the first Thanksgiving dinner the poor Pilgrims had nothing to eat but three parched grains of corn. Then the Indians came and brought them turkeys, so the Pilgrims were thankful.

Now, after they had eaten their good, big Thanksgiving dinner, Laura and Mary could eat their grains of corn and remember the Pilgrims. Parched corn was good. It crackled and crunched, and its taste was sweet and brown.

THE FEAST

The above is Laura Ingalls Wilder's description of
Thanksgiving when she was a little girl in *On the Banks
of Plum Creek*, the fourth book in the *Little House
on the Prairie* series. It was customary for a number
of years, particularly in New England, to have a few
kernels of parched corn at Thanksgiving as a reminder of
the suffering the Puritans endured.

Wilder's description relies on a mythologized version of
the event; still, a few grains of parched corn would be
a wonderful conversation starter at the Thanksgiving
table. They could also serve as a reminder of the
hardships that the first settlers had to overcome and the
generosity of the indigenous peoples toward them. This
can heighten our gratitude for the many things we have
and also inspire us to share our bounty with those less
fortunate.

Parched corn is dried corn that has been roasted. The drying preserves it, and
the roasting brings out a slightly nutty flavor that compliments the sweetness
of the corn. It's easy to make, but does take time, so do this in advance.

The first step to parched corn is to dry it. The corn may be dried on or off the
cob. If removed first, you will lose the germ of the kernels. To dry on the cob,
hang cobs by the husk in a dry place for several weeks, like the Wampanoag
and Puritans would have done.

Alternatively, you can dry the corn in the oven. To do so, cut the corn kernels
from the cob and spread in a single layer on a baking pan. You could even use
frozen corn. Place in 150° oven with the door slightly ajar for several hours,
stirring every hour or so to ensure even drying and prevent burning. Of course
you can use a dehydrator, or simply purchase dried corn, too.

Once the corn is dried, it will keep for a long time, so you don't have to be in a
hurry to parch it; but parched corn will keep for months, too, so you can move
to the next step as soon as you wish.

Heat a heavy skillet (cast iron works best) over low heat. Some people add a
bit of oil in the pan, but it's not required. Drop in a small handful of dried corn

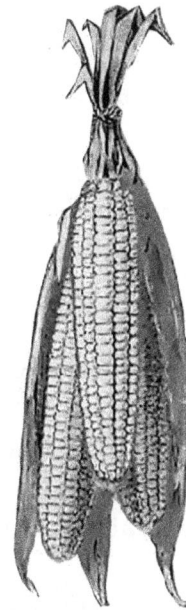

kernels and sprinkle with salt if desired. Shake the skillet frequently. Some of the kernels may pop; that's okay. Others won't, and that's fine, too. When the kernels are a nice golden brown, they're done.

To replicate the experience of parched corn at the First Thanksgiving, no seasoning should be added, with the possible exception of salt. Otherwise, you can season parched corn in any way you'd season popcorn.

HOMEMADE STOCK

You will need turkey or chicken stock to make good dressing and gravy. Other dishes may also call for stock. For best results, make your own. It can be prepared ahead of time and frozen until ready to use.

Begin by roasting about 5 pounds of turkey or chicken. You can usually get legs, necks, and wings inexpensively in the early part of November to use for stock; or you can get a 5-pound bird. Wash the meat if necessary, and pat dry. Place in a roasting or baking pan (make sure it has sides, to catch the juices) and cover with foil. Roast at 375º for 1 hour.

Place the meat in a large stockpot, and pour the drippings from the pan over them. Be sure to scrape the pan well; that's where much of the flavor comes from. Add a large chopped onion, a couple of chopped carrots, and a chopped stalk of celery. Drop in 4 sprigs each fresh parsley and thyme and a bay leaf or two. Cover well with water. Bring to a boil, then reduce heat and simmer 3 hours.

Cool enough to strain. Cool completely if not using immediately, and store in refrigerator up to 3 days, or freezer up to 3 weeks.

The strained-out meat and vegetables may be used in other dishes, such as soup or Thanksgiving Shepherd's Pie, or discarded.

...good company, good wine, good welcome, can make good people. ~William Shakespeare

TURKEY

Turkey is so much a part of Thanksgiving that the day is often referred to as "turkey day." Before deciding to cook a turkey, make sure you have the space and the equipment you'll need. Your refrigerator should have enough room to accommodate the bird; so should your oven. You'll need a pan large enough to hold the turkey. To keep the turkey from sticking to the pan, you'll also need a rack to put in the pan that holds the bird off the bottom. The easiest way to do this is to get a roasting pan with rack; you can purchase a disposable aluminum roasting pan with a rack if you are short on kitchen storage space. If you want to brine the turkey (see below), you'll also need a pot or food-safe bucket large enough to completely submerge the bird. A meat thermometer should be used.

First, thaw out the turkey if it's frozen. To do this, just place it in the refrigerator for a few days (rule of thumb: one day for every 5 pounds of meat). Alternatively, place it in cold water and change the water every half hour until the bird is no longer frozen.

The day before roasting, you can brine the turkey. This adds flavor, as well as helps the bird retain moisture so the meat will be juicier. Take the turkey out of the fridge and remove all the packaging. Reach into the bird from both ends to remove the package of giblets (and anything else that may be in there). Put the turkey in a pot or food-safe bucket large enough that you will be able to entirely submerge your turkey. (Make sure the pot will fit in the refrigerator; or, use a cooler.)

Dissolve a cup of salt in a gallon of water. You can heat the water to dissolve the salt faster, but it shouldn't get too hot to put your finger in. Pour this over the turkey, adding more water if needed to cover the bird completely. You can put a sliced onion and a sliced lemon in the pot for extra flavor. Place something heavy, like a large bowl or plate, on the turkey to hold it down if it floats. Put it in the refrigerator or in a cooler of ice overnight. An hour before roasting, pour off the salt water and rinse the turkey well. Pat it dry with paper towels and let it sit at room temperature on the rack in the roasting pan for a half to one hour.

If you can't or don't want to brine the turkey, then leave it in the refrigerator until about thirty minutes to an hour before roasting. Take the turkey out of

the fridge and remove all the packaging. Reach into the bird from both ends to remove the giblets. Set the turkey in the roasting pan on the rack with the breast side up. If it's moist, pat dry with a paper towel.

Put the oven rack on the bottom space and turn the oven on to 425° to preheat. At this point you can truss the turkey if you wish to keep the legs and wings close to the body, but it's not necessary.

Now it's time to make your seasoning mixture. Peel and crush a clove a garlic. Zest one lemon. Mix these with 2 teaspoons salt (but don't add salt if you brined the turkey!), 1 teaspoon black pepper, and 2 tablespoons each parsley, sage, rosemary and thyme – just like the song. If using dried herbs, use 2 teaspoons instead of tablespoons. Mix into a cup of real butter or coconut oil.

Rub the seasoning all over the turkey. You can rub some under the skin where you can get your fingers under it. You can also rub some inside. Put some onion slices, garlic cloves, and lemon slices in the turkey. Throw in some orange slices, cranberries, and bay leaves if that sounds good to you.

How do you know when to start roasting the turkey? Math. Allow 12 minutes per pound for roasting, although it may be done sooner.

If you have a V-rack, place your turkey breast side down on the V-rack in the roasting pan. This will allow the juices to run into the breast and help keep it moist. Otherwise, place breast side up on the regular rack in the roasting pan. Pour 2 to 4 cups of broth (or water) in the bottom of the roasting pan. The amount depends on the depth of the pan, and how much gravy you'll need.

Put the turkey in the oven and reduce heat to 350°. After 45 minutes, remove from the oven. If you've started roasting breast down, remove the V-rack and place the turkey on the regular rack breast up. Spoon up some broth from the pan and drizzle over the turkey, repeating as necessary to ensure the whole bird is basted. Return to oven.

Every 30-45 minutes, remove the turkey from the oven and repeat the basting. In the last 45 minutes or so of cooking, you can also baste the turkey with melted butter or oil. This helps crisp up the skin and turn it a nice, deep, golden brown. Continue roasting until the internal temperature is 160°. If the bird gets too brown before reaching this temperature, cover with a tent of foil.

THE SATURDAY
EVENING POST

An Illustrated Weekly
Founded A? D? by Benj. Franklin

NOVEMBER 16, 1912

T H A N K S G I V I N G

When the turkey is done, remove from oven. Lift the top up first and allow all the juice to drain off and out of the bird into the roasting pan. Save these drippings.

Place turkey on a platter (lined with kale or other greens, if desired) and cover with a tent of foil. Let it sit for about 20 minutes. During this time you can enhance the presentation by garnishing the platter around the turkey. Possibilities include sprigs of herbs, cranberries, nuts, citrus, edible blooms, or whatever strikes your fancy.

What if you get up Thanksgiving morning and realize the turkey is still frozen, or partially frozen? You will roast as above with two differences. Set the oven at 325°, and keep it that temperature for the entire roasting time. It will take about 18 minutes per pound from fully frozen to done. Partially frozen birds will take less time. The wings will get done first, followed by the legs. You may want to cover those parts with foil as they reach 160° so they don't burn before the rest of the bird is done.

Don't season a frozen bird; just sprinkle with salt and pepper. Once the outside is thawed, spread with herbed butter and continue cooking.

That's the most popular way to cook turkey for Thanksgiving. I did that, too, for a couple of years, but decided I wanted a tastier, moister meat on my platter. So, I started getting a smoked turkey—not lunch meat-style formed stuff, but a whole, truly-smoked bird. Mesquite-smoked is most flavorful, but hickory or any other flavor is also good.

Being smoked, it's already cooked and ready to eat; all you have to do is heat it up. It can be heated whole and carried in and served in a Norman-Rockwell-painting manner. Or, it can be carved ahead of time; then you heat only what you need for the dinner. That's what I do, and it saves much time, effort, and oven space. It also makes the leftovers fresher, because they're not really left over, but prepared when needed. If you get a smoked turkey, it's important to remember to save the juices in the wrapping when you open it. These will be the drippings you'll need later to make gravy.

Deep-fried turkey is becoming more popular. With a special fryer, this method saves your oven for the other dishes. And anything fried is tasty. To cook a turkey this way, follow the directions that come with the fryer.

Don't forget to let the two youngest people at the table (who are able) break the wishbone, making a secret wish as they do.

Will you be alone, or with a very small party on Thanksgiving? There's no need to miss out on the feast just because you don't want to prepare a whole turkey. Roast a Cornish game hen per person. The process is the same, but it takes only about an hour or so to roast a hen (or small pan of hens).

GRAVY

The drippings you had left from the roast turkey (or the package of the smoked turkey) are what you'll use to make the gravy. Have everything at hand because it goes quickly.

For best results, heat the stock before beginning. The consistency of the gravy will be smoother.

Heat the drippings in a skillet on the stovetop over low heat until hot. (If you roasted a turkey and your roasting pan fits on your stove top, you can remove the turkey and make the gravy in the same pan.) Have your whisk handy, and slowly sprinkle in an equal amount of flour into the hot drippings, whisking all the while. Continue whisking until the flour is browned, about 2 to 3 minutes.

Slowly pour in broth, a cup at a time, whisking all the while, looking for lumps to break up. Allow to come to a simmer, still whisking, before adding the next cup of stock. Continue to add stock, whisking all the while, and heat until it is almost the consistency you want. It will thicken more as it sits, so don't overdo it now.

If you've used a smoked turkey or seasoned broth, no additional seasoning is necessary; otherwise, salt and pepper to taste.

For East Texas-style gravy like Nanny made, use less broth and whisk in a cup of milk. Then, have some slices of boiled egg, some sautéed onion slices, and some cooked giblets ready to stir into the gravy before serving.

DRESSING

Only real southern cornbread dressing will do for my family. So the first thing you need to do is make cornbread. For the best-textured dressing, make the cornbread a day—or even two—ahead of time. Here's how to do it:

Mix together in a medium sized bowl:
1 cup flour
1 cup stone ground corn meal
1 teaspoon salt
1 tablespoon baking powder

In a small bowl, beat 2 eggs. Whisk in 1 cup milk, 1/4 cup oil, and 1 tablespoon pure maple syrup (don't use a commercially-made "flavored" syrup, but you can use honey, agave nectar, sugar, etc.).

Stir wet ingredients into dry. The more you stir it, the fluffier it will be, so if you don't want it too cake-like, stir just until mixed.

Pour into a buttered pan. If you like thin cornbread use a 9" x 11" pan; for thicker cornbread use an 8- or 9-inch pan. Bake at 400° for 20 minutes or until nicely browned on top and an inserted toothpick comes out clean.

Remove from oven and cool completely. Wrap in a clean, dry towel and let sit overnight.

Also the day before making the dressing, boil 4 eggs, and chop 2 bunches green onion, half a bunch of celery, and about a cup of chopped cooked turkey or giblets. This is another reason I carve the turkey ahead of time – no one can see that I robbed it for the dressing. If you want to serve a whole turkey, you can either use the neck and giblets that you pull out of the turkey (be sure to cook them first), or purchase some extra turkey to use in the dressing.

To make the dressing, crumble the cornbread in a large bowl and stir in the chopped vegetables, eggs, and turkey. Sprinkle in 2 tablespoons poultry seasoning, 2 teaspoons salt, and 2 teaspoons pepper and stir. Then stir chicken broth into it, a cup or so at a time, until it's soggy throughout.

If you're making it ahead of time, stop at this point and store the dressing in an airtight container in the refrigerator up to two days or the freezer up to a month. If frozen, remove from freezer the day before baking. Continue as below.

Dump into a well-greased and floured baking or roasting pan and shake the pan so the dressing spreads evenly, but don't press down. Cover, but leave corner vented, and bake about an hour, checking occasionally to be sure it's not getting burnt on bottom or too dried out. If it is, take it out and stir well, then recover with vent and continue baking. You can even add more broth if needed. It may not take a full hour; it depends on your oven and how dry you like the dressing. In our home, dressing is meant to put gravy on, so we like it on the dry side to absorb more gravy. Some people like moist or even soggy dressing. Since everything in it is already cooked, all you are really doing is heating it through and getting it to the level of moistness you want. Unless you like it really moist, take the cover off the last ten minutes to brown the top.

My husband's family made dressing similarly but with a couple of differences. First, they weren't sticklers for cornbread-only dressing. Nanny would usually make a small pan of cornbread (a half or quarter recipe, depending on how much she needed) and the tear up whatever other bread she had with it.

The second difference has to do with the need to stretch a little meat a long way that Nanny experienced during the Depression. Instead of a little meat chopped fine to flavor dressing as a side to the turkey, she would boil a chicken, debone it, and cut the meat into larger, chicken-tender-size pieces, and mix it into the dressing. So they actually had "chicken dressing" as the main dish instead of turkey with dressing on the side.

A vegetarian version of this dressing can be made with a few simple substitutions. Use vegetable broth instead of chicken broth, and add nuts and/or root vegetables (carrots, turnips, parsnips, etc.) in place of the turkey. When making the cornbread, substitute soy or almond milk for the dairy, and increase the oil by ¼ cup (for ½ cup total) in place of eggs.

None of our family ever made stuffing. As the name implies, stuffing is simply dressing that is stuffed into the turkey and baked along with the bird. If you try this method, be sure the stuffing reaches a temperature of at least 165°.

We can only be said to be alive in those moments when our hearts are conscious of our treasures.
~Thornton Wilder

31

GRANNY LIL'S ROAST VENISON

Venison is not as popular as fowl for Thanksgiving, but in some parts of the county, including the Texas hill country, it still makes an appearance, especially among hunting families like ours. Both my mother's and father's families often had roast venison on special occasions, including Thanksgiving. The shoulder or rump was used, and usually cooked in a slow cooker or electric roasting pan.

1 venison roast
About 8 whole garlic cloves, peeled
2 tablespoons rosemary, crushed (2 teaspoons if using dried)
2 teaspoons black pepper
1 tablespoon thyme (1 teaspoon if dried)
10 medium carrots, quartered
5 small onions, quartered
3 stalks celery, quartered
1 tablespoon flour
3 cups beef broth OR
3 cups water and 1 tablespoon beef bouillon granules

Start the day before by soaking the entire roast in buttermilk (whole milk will also work) overnight in the refrigerator. The fat in the milk absorbs any gamey odors, and the lactic acid and calcium both act as tenderizers by breaking down the proteins and softening the collagen.

Some people marinate venison and other meats in vinegar. I don't like to use vinegar for two reasons. One is that vinegar is a different and stronger type of acid, which oxidizes the myoglobin in the meat. Oxidation is unhealthy (which is why we all try to take antioxidants). It can also cause oxidation in the fat (although there's not much fat in venison), which turns it rancid. And two, the flavor of venison soaked in milk is much nicer than venison in vinegar, since it's less gamey.

After soaking, rinse the roast and pat dry. Let it sit out for 30 minutes to an hour.

Cut 8 deep slits in the roast and place a whole, peeled clove of garlic in each slit. (You may need more or less depending on the size of the roast.) Combine the spices and rub over the entire roast.

Pour about an inch of beef broth or water in the bottom of the roasting pan, and place the roast and vegetables in the pan. Cover and bake at 325° for 2- 1/2 to 3 hours, or until meat is tender. Remove meat and vegetables to a serving platter; keep warm.

Place the roasting pan on the stove over medium heat. Scrape the bottom well to get all the bits of meat off. If there's not much meaty flavor to the pan juice, and you're using water instead of beef broth, you may need to crumble in a cube of beef bouillon. This is because venison doesn't have much fat to drip down and flavor the water in the bottom of the pan. Sprinkle in a tablespoon of flour, whisking all the while. Bring to a boil, while whisking, then reduce heat to low and cook until the gravy is slightly runny (it will thicken more as it sits, so don't over-thicken now). Serve with the roast and vegetables.

STUFFED ACORN SQUASH

Some members of our family are vegetarian. We've also hosted vegan families for Thanksgiving. When we don't have turkey, we enjoy stuffed and baked acorn squash as a satisfying main dish. It can also be baked as a side dish.

As an added bonus, the squash may be baked and stuffed the day before and refrigerated. On Thanksgiving, it's quick and easy to reheat. Just cover the baking dish loosely with foil and place in the oven at 350º, checking every 5 minutes until it is hot.

For every 2 medium acorn squash (about 2 pounds each):
3 tablespoons apple cider vinegar
3 tablespoons olive oil
2 tablespoons pure maple syrup
Kosher salt and freshly ground black pepper
1 small onion, chopped
1 cup quinoa, rinsed well (you can use red, white, or black quinoa, or any combination)
1 teaspoon chili powder
1/2 teaspoon ground cinnamon
1/4 teaspoon cayenne pepper
1/4 cup dried cranberries
1 cup loosely packed fresh parsley leaves, chopped
1/4 cup pecans, coarsely chopped

Preheat the oven to 400°.

Cut each squash in half lengthwise and scoop out and discard the seeds. Place the halves in a large baking dish, flesh-side up.

Whisk together the vinegar, 2 tablespoons of the oil and the maple syrup in a cup. Brush the flesh of the squash halves with the maple mixture and sprinkle with salt and pepper. Put the squash flesh down in the baking dish, then brush the skin with maple mixture and sprinkle with salt and pepper. Roast on middle rack until the flesh is fork-tender, about 45 minutes to an hour.

Meanwhile, heat the remaining 1 tablespoon oil in a medium saucepan over medium-high heat. Add the onions and sauté, stirring occasionally, until soft and golden brown. Add the quinoa, chili powder, cinnamon, and 1 teaspoon salt and stir until the spices are toasted, about 1 minute.

Add 2 cups water and bring to a simmer. Reduce heat, cover and simmer, stirring occasionally, until the quinoa is tender and most of the liquid is absorbed, 20 to 25 minutes. Remove from the heat and let sit, covered, for 5 minutes. Uncover and stir in the cranberries, remaining maple mixture, half of the parsley and half of the pecans.

When the squash are done, remove from oven, turn halves over, poke the flesh with a fork, and brush with more of the maple mixture. Stuff the squash halves with the quinoa and sprinkle with the remaining parsley and pecans. Serve warm.

NANNY'S SQUASH CASSEROLE

For an alternate squash dish, try this popular, post-war casserole of Nanny's.

1 tablespoon olive oil
1 onion, small diced
2 jalapeños, seeds removed and chopped
2 garlic cloves, minced
3 cups yellow squash, cut in 1/4-inch slices
1 small can diced tomatoes, drained
1 cup grated cheese
2 cups breadcrumbs and/or Ritz cracker crumbs, separated
Salt and pepper, to taste

Preheat oven to 350°F. Sauté onions and jalapeño in olive oil for about 5 minutes, or until onions are translucent. Stir in squash, garlic, tomatoes, cheese, salt, pepper, and 1 cup crumbs. Pour into well-greased casserole dish and bake until cheese is bubbly, about 40 minutes. Sprinkle remaining crumbs on top and broil just until golden.

SAUTÉED SQUASH

For a super-simple squash dish, sauté a chopped onion in butter; when translucent, add 4 chopped yellow squash (and/or zucchini squash) and continue sautéing until tender. Season to taste with salt and pepper.

MASHED POTATOES

No Thanksgiving would be complete without mashed potatoes.

Wash and peel a potato per person, plus a couple extras. Chop them up, and put in a pot; cover with water.

You can stop at this point and store the water-covered potatoes in the refrigerator overnight. The water prevents air from touching the flesh of the potato and keeps them from turning brown. The next day, pour that water off and cover with fresh water to continue.

Make sure potatoes are covered with water, about an inch over. Sprinkle liberally with salt. Bring to a boil over high heat, then reduce heat to medium-low and cook until tender. You can cook covered or uncovered, but potatoes have a habit of boiling over, so keep a close eye on them, especially if you put a lid on them.

When tender enough to easily break apart with a fork, remove from heat and drain. Add a half stick of butter and a quarter cup milk per every 4 or so potatoes. Sprinkle with salt and pepper. Mash all together and beat well.

Use a large spoon or potato masher for a home-style dish, or an electric mixer for an extra-smooth consistency. If too dry, add more milk and butter. If you want extra-white, thick and creamy potatoes, mash in 1/2 to 1 cup softened cream cheese.

Keep warm until ready to serve.

COLCANNON

A unique way to enjoy potatoes on Thanksgiving is Colcannon, a traditional dish from Ireland. This recipe is from the Irish side of my family.

1 1/2 pounds russet potatoes
1 savoy cabbage
1 leek

Remember God's bounty in the year... Give this one day to thanks, to joy, to gratitude!
~Henry Ward Beecher

1 cup milk
2 tablespoons butter plus 1 more
1/4 teaspoon freshly grated nutmeg
Salt and pepper

Preheat broiler. Peel and quarter potatoes. Cover with cold water in medium saucepan and sprinkle generously with salt. Bring to a boil, then reduce heat and simmer until tender, about 15 minutes. Drain potatoes and return to saucepan; mash. Cover and set aside, keeping warm.

Meanwhile, in another saucepan, combine remaining ingredients. Season with salt and pepper to taste. Cover and cook over medium heat, stirring occasionally, just until cabbage and leek are soft, about 15 minutes.

Stir warm potatoes into cabbage mixture. Spread into 8" baking pan or casserole dish. Place under broiler about 5 minutes, until lightly browned.

Remove from broiler and top with a pat of butter. Serve immediately.

SWEET POTATOES

Thanksgiving is one of the few times it's traditional to have both white and sweet potatoes at the same meal. Butternut squash could also be used in this recipe.

First, cook the sweet potatoes. Usually, 1 sweet potato per adult is all you need, unless they're unusually small; then you can add a couple extra. You can boil or microwave them, and you can peel them before or after cooking.

When very tender, break into pieces with a fork, or mash them, depending on how you like them. For every four yams, stir in a stick of butter, 1/2 cup brown sugar, 1/2 cup pecans, and 1/2 teaspoon cinnamon. Mix until butter and sugar are melted and spread throughout.

Spread the mashed sweet potatoes into a well-buttered baking dish. Cover with marshmallows and brown at the last minute. Or leave the marshmallows off. The potatoes are plenty sweet without them.

GREEN BEAN CASSEROLE

For exceptionally good green bean casserole, fry some home-made onion rings, make a rich, creamy mushroom sauce from scratch, and use fresh green beans you've already cooked. The recipes for these things follow; however, this is the one dish I will take shortcuts with, so there's a quick and easy way first.

Quick and easy:

1 can cream of mushroom soup
2 cans French-cut green beans, drained
3/4 cup milk
Salt and pepper
1 can fried onions

Mix soup with green beans and milk. Sprinkle liberally with black pepper. Stir in 3/4 can of fried onions and spread into a well-greased casserole dish. Bake covered at 400° until hot and bubbly, about 20 minutes, then uncover and sprinkle the remaining fried onions on top. Bake uncovered another ten minutes, or until the top onions are golden brown and crispy.

The best way:

First, make the onion rings. They can be made up to 2 days ahead of time.

1 whole 1015 (large, sweet, yellow) onion
2 cups buttermilk
2 cups flour
1 tablespoon salt
1/4 teaspoon cayenne pepper
1 quart Canola oil

Slice the onion into thin rounds. Place in a baking dish, cover with buttermilk, and soak for at least an hour.

Heat oil in small fryer or large kettle or Dutch oven to 375°.

Combine dry ingredients in a gallon size plastic storage bag, seal, and shake. Add onion rings to flour mixture and shake to coat. Take out a few at a time, shaking slightly to remove excess. Drop one at a time into hot oil. Fry until golden brown; remove with slotted spoon and place on a plate lined with several layers of paper towels. Repeat with remaining onions. Cool completely. Store in an airtight container until ready to use.

Prepare the green beans:

Trim the ends off 2 pounds of green beans, pulling strings off as necessary. Snap beans into pieces 2" – 3" long. Rinse well and place in a large pot. Cover with cold water and salt liberally. Bring to a boil, and cook about 15 minutes, until they reach desired tenderness. If you like them crisp, 5 minutes will be enough; for very tender beans, it may take 20 minutes. When done, drain and set aside. The beans can be cooked a day or two ahead of time; let cool completely, then cover and store in refrigerator until ready to use, and reheat.

When you're ready to make the casserole:

6 tablespoons butter, divided
1 pound button mushrooms, cleaned and diced
1- 1/2 cups sliced shallots
4 cloves garlic, peeled and minced
1 cup whole milk
1 cup half and half
1 cup chicken stock
6 tablespoons flour
1 teaspoon ground mustard powder
Salt and pepper to taste
1/2 cup grated cheddar cheese

In a large skillet, melt 2 tablespoons of butter on medium-high heat. Add the onion and sauté 5 minutes. Add the mushrooms, garlic, and a pinch of salt. Continue cooking, stirring often, until mushrooms are soft, about 5 minutes.

Add the remaining 4 tablespoons butter to the skillet and melt over medium-low heat. Whisk the flour into the skillet and cook on low heat for about 2 minutes.

Combine the milk, half and half, and chicken stock. Pour into the skillet and continue cooking, whisking until thickened, about 10 minutes. Stir in mustard powder, and a generous amount of salt and pepper.

Simmer about 5 minutes. Taste and adjust the seasoning as desired. Stir the green beans into the mushroom sauce and toss to combine. If you have plenty of onion rings, stir some into the mixture. Pour into a large, buttered casserole dish. Bake uncovered for 15 minutes. Add the grated cheddar to the top and bake another 10 minutes or until the cheese melts. Top with onion rings and bake uncovered for 5 more minutes. Let stand for 10 minutes before serving.

VEGAN GREEN BEAN CASSEROLE

When we have vegan guests, this green bean casserole lets them enjoy the dish along with everyone else. It's so good, most people don't realize it's vegan.

2 pounds green beans
Salt and pepper to taste
4 tablespoons margarine or olive oil
2 shallots, minced
4 cloves garlic, minced
2 cups finely-chopped mushrooms
4 tablespoons flour
1- 1/2 cups vegetable broth
2 cups unsweetened, unflavored almond milk
3 cups crispy fried onions

Cook the beans as above.

Meanwhile, sauté shallots and garlic in margarine or olive oil over medium heat for 3 minutes. Add mushrooms and cook 5 minutes more.

Sprinkle in flour and whisk to stir and coat the veggies. Cook for 1 minute, then slowly drizzle in vegetable stock, whisking continuously.

Whisk in almond milk. Season with salt and pepper and simmer on low heat until it's thick and bubbly. Taste and adjust seasonings as needed.

Remove from heat and toss in ½ cup of the fried onions and all of the cooked green beans. Pour into well-greased casserole dish. Top with remaining fried onions and bake at 400° for 15 minutes, or until bubbly and slightly browned on top.

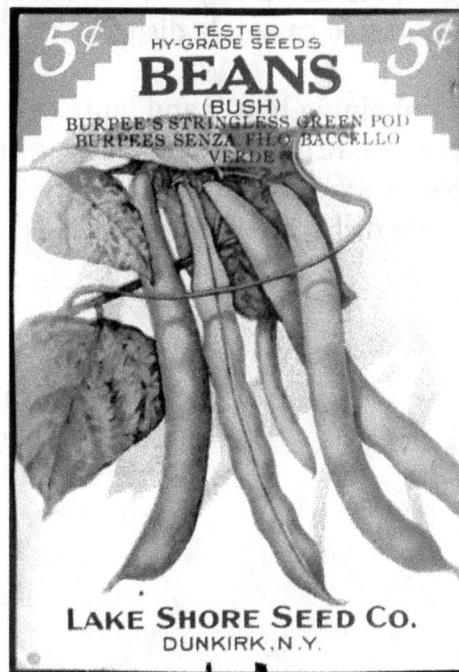

SCALLOPED OYSTERS

Certain dishes are popular regionally. While we in the south never thought of having oysters for Thanksgiving, when an uncle married a lady from the north, we learned that many people can't imagine the dinner without them.

6 tablespoons unsalted butter, divided
3 cups coarse fresh breadcrumbs
1/4 teaspoon each salt and pepper
1/4 cup coarsely chopped fresh flat-leaf parsley
1 celery stalk, thinly sliced
3 scallions, trimmed and chopped
2 teaspoons fresh thyme leaves
3/4 cup heavy cream
2 pints shucked fresh oysters in their liquor
1/8 teaspoon freshly grated nutmeg

Preheat oven to 450°. Drain oysters, reserving 2 tablespoons of the liquid.

Melt 2 tablespoons butter over medium heat. Add 1/4 teaspoon salt and the breadcrumbs. Stirring frequently, cook until crumbs are crisp, about 10 minutes. Stir in parsley. Remove from heat. Sprinkle half the crumbs in a large, well-buttered casserole dish.

Melt remaining butter and sauté celery and scallions 2 minutes. Stir in thyme. Add cream. Bring to a boil and stir in reserved oyster liquor, nutmeg, and pepper. Remove from heat and stir in oysters. Spread over breadcrumbs in casserole dish; top with remaining crumbs. Bake until bubbly, about 8 minutes.

Let the thankful heart
sweep through the day
and, as the magnet finds the iron,
so it will find, in every hour,
some heavenly blessings!
~Henry Ward Beecher

CRANBERRY SAUCE

12 oz. fresh cranberries
3/4 cup sugar
1 tablespoon orange zest
Rest of the peel from the orange, cut into strips
1/2 cup freshly-squeezed orange juice
1 stick cinnamon

Pick over cranberries to remove any bad berries and stems. Rinse remaining cranberries and place in a saucepan with remaining ingredients. Cover and cook 15 minutes over medium heat, stirring frequently. When cranberries have all popped, remove from heat.

When cool, remove orange peel and cinnamon stick. The sauce will thicken as it sits; if it gets too thick, stir in a bit of water.

Store covered in refrigerator. This can be made a day or two ahead of time.

SUGARED CRANBERRIES

While you have the fresh cranberries out, sugar some for use in pies and other dishes, or just to snack on. This is a two-day process, but worth it.

1 cup fresh cranberries
2 cups sugar
1 cup water

Make a simple syrup by bringing 1 cup sugar and 1 cup water to a boil, whisking until the sugar is dissolved. Remove from heat and cool 5 minutes. Stir cranberries into the syrup and place in refrigerator overnight.

The next morning, drain the cranberries (the syrup will be very thick) and sprinkle with 1 cup of sugar. Toss cranberries until all are coated. Spread on waxed paper and allow to dry at least 2 hours.

Store in an air-tight container. Use sugared cranberries to accent pumpkin & apple pie and other dishes, or for snacking.

Give thanks for a little and you will find a lot. ~Hansa Proverb

PINTO BEANS

Pinto beans are not a traditional Thanksgiving dish, but they should be; beans were one of the "three sisters" staple foods. My family—on either dad's side or mom's side—never got together for any kind of meal without pinto beans.

The day before cooking, pick over a package of pinto beans and remove any bad ones. Cover remaining beans with water and let sit overnight. Be sure to use plenty of water; the beans will soak it up, and if there's not enough water some of the beans will be hard. There should be a couple of inches of water over them.

The next morning, pour off the soaking water and rinse beans well.

Place in a large pot and cover with fresh water, at least an inch over.

Most people prefer the flavor of beans cooked with ham. A smoked ham hock can be added to the beans if you wish.

Bring to a boil, then reduce heat so that beans will just simmer. Put a lid on the saucepot, but leave it ajar. It will take at least two or three hours to cook the beans thoroughly, and can take several hours if the beans were old. Stir occasionally. Alternatively, you can cook them in a covered slow cooker overnight.

When the beans begin to get tender, add 1 bunch chopped cilantro, and salt, pepper, garlic powder, and chili powder to taste.

The beans can be cooked as early as Monday and heated up for Thanksgiving dinner. If you cook/reheat them in a slow cooker, it will save stove space for other dishes.

CORN

Corn was the other one of the "three sisters." You can use fresh, frozen, or canned corn for an easy side dish appropriate for Thanksgiving.

Simply melt 2 tablespoons butter in a pot; add the corn and toss to coat. Pepper liberally and heat until warm.

CREAMED CORN

For a more Southern taste, cream the corn.

1 quart corn
1 cup milk
1 tablespoon sugar
1/2 teaspoon pepper
8 ounces cream cheese, cubed
1/2 cup (1 stick) butter, cut into thin slices

If preparing on the stovetop, mix all together in a saucepot and stir frequently until the butter and cheese are melted and heated through.

Or, place corn into a slow cooker. Stir in milk, sugar and pepper until well combined. Top with butter and cream cheese. Cover and cook on high heat for 2 - 3 hours. Uncover and stir until butter and cream cheese are well combined. Cover and cook on high heat for an additional 15 minutes.

ROASTED ROOTS & COBS

For a heartier corn dish, add root vegetables and roast.

1 pound each carrots and parsnips, cut into 1- 1/2" circles
1 pound turnips, cut into 1" chunks
1- 1/2 pounds corn on the cob, cut into 2" pieces
1/3 cup olive oil
1 tablespoon rosemary
1 teaspoon finely minced garlic
Salt and pepper to taste

Preheat oven to 400º. Pour olive oil into a large (11" x 17") sheet pan.

Place vegetables in the olive oil, sprinkle with seasonings, and toss, then spread vegetables evenly in the pan. Place on middle oven rack and roast 35 to 40 minutes, until tender.

Squeeze lemon juice over the vegetables before serving for a pop of freshness.

BRUSSELS SPROUTS

Extra vegetables (especially green ones) are always welcome. Brussels sprouts go well with turkey and dressing. They may be roasted, or put in a salad for some freshness at the table.

ROASTED SPROUTS

1 pound Brussels sprouts, washed, ends trimmed, and cut in half
3 cloves minced garlic
1 teaspoon lemon juice
2 tablespoons olive oil
Salt, pepper to taste
1/4 cup sliced almonds, pine nuts, sunflower seeds, or chopped pecans
Optional: ¼ cup freshly-grated Parmesan cheese

Preheat oven to 400°.

In a large bowl, toss the sprouts with garlic, lemon juice, and olive oil. Sprinkle very generously with salt and pepper.

Spread on baking sheet or oven-proof skillet (like cast iron) in a single layer. Place on top rack of oven and roast for 20 to 30 minutes until nicely browned.

Sprinkle with nuts/seeds and cheese while hot, and serve immediately.

THANKSGIVING-DRESSED SPOUT-KALE SALAD

Start by zesting one orange. Set the zest aside. Juice the orange, and combine with the following ingredients for the dressing:

1 tablespoon olive oil
1 teaspoon Dijon mustard
1 clove garlic
1 green onion, washed and trimmed
1/4 teaspoon salt
1/4 teaspoon pepper
1/4 teaspoon cinnamon

Blend or process until smooth. Pour into a small container and refrigerate until ready to serve the salad.

For the salad:

Wash and trim 1 pound of Brussels sprouts and 1 bunch kale. Chop well.

Toss together with the orange zest, 1/2 cup dried (or sugared – see page 43) cranberries, and 1/2 cup pecans. (Optional: 1/2 cup crumbled feta cheese.)

When ready to serve, shake dressing to blend, drizzle over salad, and toss.

ANGEL BISCUITS

Angel biscuits are a cross between a dinner roll and a biscuit, as they use both yeast and baking powder as leavening. As such, they are a little more forgiving than regular biscuits, but have the taste and texture of a biscuit when hot and the softness of a yeast roll when they've cooled.

The secret to making good biscuits is a light touch. The more the dough is handled, the tougher the biscuits will be.

1/2 cup lukewarm water
1 teaspoon instant yeast
2- 1/2 cups flour
2 tablespoons sugar
1 teaspoon salt
2 teaspoons baking powder
1/4 cup vegetable shortening, chilled*
1/4 cup (4 tablespoons) butter, cold*
1/2 cup milk or buttermilk at room temperature

*You can use 1/2 cup butter instead of 1/4 cup each shortening and butter. If you do this, freeze for an hour before baking for best results.

*Alternatively, you can use 1/2 cup shortening instead of 1/4 cup each shortening and butter. The biscuits will rise higher but won't be as flavorful.

In a small mixing bowl, whisk together the warm water, yeast and 1/4 cup of the flour. Set the mixture aside for 30 minutes.

In a medium-sized bowl, whisk together the remaining flour, the sugar, salt, and baking powder. Cut in the shortening and the butter until crumbly.

Add the milk to the yeast mixture, and pour this all at once into the dry ingredients. Fold together gently but quickly until the mixture leaves the sides of the bowl and becomes cohesive. Sprinkle with an additional tablespoon of cold water only if necessary to make the dough hold together.

Turn the dough out onto a floured work surface. Pat it gently to about 3/4" thick. Cut the dough into 2" round biscuits. Gather, re-roll (handling as little as possible) and cut the leftover dough.

Place the biscuits on a greased baking sheet. Cover with a clean, dry dishtowel, and allow them to rise for 1 hour in a warm room, or overnight in the refrigerator.

You can make the dough ahead of time and store the unbaked biscuits in a plastic storage bag in the freezer. Bake as usual when ready.

When ready to bake, preheat the oven to 400°. Place biscuits on baking pan, close together. Bake on top oven rack until golden brown on top and bottom, about 10 to 12 minutes.

Baked biscuits may be frozen for up to a month and reheated to serve; however, they will not be quite as tender as usual.

GRANNY'S SALAD PICKLES

A pickle and/or olive tray makes an appearance on many Thanksgiving tables. While you have to plan pretty far in advance to have homemade pickles and relish, these pickles and the following relish are worth it.

Granny's Salad Pickles are a blue-ribbon-recipe from my mother's side of the family. As kids, my friends would sometimes come over just to have a snack – as long as it was these pickles. My cousin and I have been known to eat an entire quart in one sitting. They're that good.

40 large pickling cucumbers
3 large white onions
1 cup salt
10 cups white vinegar
10 cups sugar
4 tablespoons mustard seed
2 teaspoon turmeric

Wash cucumbers and slice as thinly as possible. Chop onion and combine with cucumber and salt. Let stand 3 hours then drain.

Combine remaining ingredients in large kettle and bring to a boil. Add drained cucumbers and onions; boil 2 to 3 minutes (no more!). Pack loosely into jars and seal.

Makes 8 quarts (or 16 pints). The recipe can easily be halved.

NANNY'S SUNSHINE RELISH

Nanny's Sunshine Relish has been a closely-guarded secret in my husband's family for generations. It has won numerous blue ribbons at various county fairs in at least two states, Tennessee and Texas. Dozens of people have requested jars of it for Christmas gifts. I'm sharing it now because it deserves to be enjoyed as much as possible.

10 cups chopped yellow squash
1 chopped white or small yellow onion
1 green bell pepper
1 red bell pepper
2 tablespoons salt
1 teaspoon turmeric
1 teaspoon alum
1 teaspoon mustard seed
1 teaspoon celery seed
3 cups sugar
2 cups vinegar

Mix vegetables with salt, cover with cold water, and let stand 1 hour, then drain.

In a large saucepot, mix vinegar, sugar and spices. Bring to a boil, and stir in drained vegetables. Return to a full boil, then immediately pack into jars and seal.

For a variation, you can use 2 or 3 jalapeños in place of green bell peppers. If you remove the seeds, but leave the white "walls" on the inside of the peppers, you will have a medium-heat relish, and if you add the seeds with the peppers you will have a hot relish.

We called the various heats Sunshine (for no heat), Sunny (for medium heat) and Blazing Sun (for hot). For Scorching, add a habanero pepper, but don't let children have this, and have milk handy for those who aren't aware of how much scorch a habanero has.

Note that if you ever see any kind of "Sunshine Relish" in the store, as I have, it's not this.

FRUIT SALAD

Both sides of my family always had fruit salad at Thanksgiving. The crystal bowl I inherited from Granny was brought from Germany by her great grandmother, and was always used to hold the fruit salad on special occasions.

Granny made the simplest fruit salad. She chopped 2 red apples, broke 2 oranges into sections and cut each section into halves or thirds, and sliced 3 bananas. She sprinkled a little lemon juice and sugar over it, stirred, and put it in the refrigerator until the meal was nearly done.

The fruit salad was served at the end of the meal, but before dessert. This was probably an attempt to get a few more nutrients into people with a little fruit before they gorged themselves on pies.

Granny Lil made a similar fruit salad, but she used pineapple instead of oranges. You can use a can of pineapple chunks, but it won't as good as if you use fresh. Don't be intimidated; it's easy to chop a pineapple. Just follow these steps:

Lay the fruit on its side and cut off the top and bottom. Then stand it up and slice the peel off from top to bottom. Next, while the pineapple is still standing, cut it in half top to bottom. Lay each half down and cut into wedges, then chop the wedges crosswise into chunks.

Granny Lil would also add other fruits, depending on what she had on hand. Maraschino cherries were often present. Sometimes she would cut up some home-canned pears and/or peaches into the salad. (Thanksgiving is not peach season, so fresh ones – if you can even find them at that time of year – wouldn't have any flavor; store-bought canned peaches aren't as good, but could be used.)

NANNY'S AMBROSIA

While my family made simple fruit salads, my husband's mother got a little fancier with Ambrosia. The grandkids could never get enough.

1 cup pineapple, cut into small chunks
3 Clementine or mandarin oranges, sectioned and de-seeded
3/4 cup maraschino cherries, drained
1 cup shredded coconut
1 cup miniature marshmallow
1/2 cup coarsely chopped pecans
3- 1/2 cups whipped cream

Mix fruit, marshmallows, and pecans in bowl. Add whipped cream and fold fruit mixture in until well incorporated. Serve chilled.

MULLED APPLE CIDER

6 cups unfiltered apple juice or cider
1 orange
12 cloves
3 large cinnamon sticks (or 6 small sticks)
1/3 cup sugar

Use a skewer to poke 12 holes around the top of the orange. Stick a clove into each hole. Slice orange so that all the cloves are around one slice; then slice remainder of the orange.

Combine all ingredients in a heavy saucepan. Bring to simmer over medium heat. Do not boil. Reduce heat to low and cook 5 minutes. Remove and discard orange slices and cinnamon sticks. Serve hot.

BUTTERED CIDER

6 cups apple unfiltered apple juice or cider
1/3 cup packed brown sugar
1/4 cup butter
1/4 cup honey
1/4 teaspoon cinnamon
1/4 teaspoon nutmeg

Beat everything except the juice/cider until well-blended and fluffy. This can be made up to 2 weeks before Thanksgiving. Bring to room temperature before using.

Heat apple juice/cider in a heavy saucepan over medium heat until hot but not boiling. Fill cups or mugs with juice/cider and stir in 1 tablespoon of butter mixture per cup.

Happiness doesn't come as a result of getting something we don't have, but rather of recognizing and appreciating what we do have. ~ Frederick Keonig

A NOTE ABOUT ALCOHOLIC BEVERAGES

The decision to serve alcohol is a personal one. If you do serve any alcohol, or allow guests to bring their own, here are a few things you might want to keep in mind.

Will anyone who is drinking need a designated driver or a taxi/car service later? Make plans ahead of time if possible by knowing what services are available in your area and how to reach them.

If it's your first time hosting, you might not have had to deal with someone over-indulging to the point of becoming disruptive or otherwise problematic, so it may be helpful to think ahead of time about what you would do if that happens. Is there a person you can ask for help?

Not everyone will wish to drink alcoholic beverages. People may choose to abstain for various reasons – religion, fighting an addiction, pregnancy, or maybe they just don't want to imbibe at that time. Sometimes well-intentioned people may overly "encourage" others to have a drink; if this happens, you can step in with a reminder of the other options available.

This is especially true if there are toasts. A nondrinker can feel either left out or conspicuous during toasts if they don't have a glass to raise. Having a glass of water at each place in addition to the alcoholic beverage when toasts are made can help avoid hurt feelings.

A NOTE ABOUT DIETS

No one should feel pressured to eat any particular thing(s). The feast is before them; let each person choose what and how much of it to have. Trying to persuade someone to have something they do not want is not only unkind, but it could be dangerous to their health. If you see someone being coaxed, step in and guide the conversation another way.

MIMI'S PIE CRUST

This is the pie crust I use for every pie, including the blue ribbon winners. It makes enough for two crusts (a top and bottom for one pie, or the bottom crust for two open-top pies). This pie crust pastry can each be made up to 3 months in advance and kept in the freezer until ready to use. If using frozen, place in the refrigerator the day before use to thaw.

The secret to good pie crust is keeping two things to a minimum: heat and handling. For best results, be sure the shortening and butter are well chilled. Nanny always put the dry ingredients in the freezer for an hour or so, too. She put the bowl and knives (or pastry cutter, if you have one of the new-fangled things) in the refrigerator to chill as well. When mixing, do it quickly but gently, and as little as possible.

3 cups flour
1/2 cup shortening, chilled
1/2 cup butter, chilled
1 teaspoon salt
1 tablespoon sugar
1 egg lightly beaten, divided
1 tablespoon lemon juice (or vinegar)
1/3 cup ice water
1 tablespoon milk

Measure flour, shortening, butter, salt, sugar, and 1/2 of egg into mixing bowl. Use two knives or pastry blender to cut together until mixture resembles a coarse meal. Stir in lemon juice. Sprinkle ice water over mixture a little at a time, using just enough to gather into a ball that holds together. Wrap in plastic, refrigerate to chill.

For two single-crust pies, divide evenly. If making a two-crust pie, separate a little less than half the mixture for the bottom crust, and the remaining for the top crust.

Roll on floured surface or between waxed paper into a circle large enough to line the pie pan. Sprinkle a little flour on the bottom of the pie pan (or spritz lightly with cooking oil) before placing the crust in the pan. Pre-bake crust if required, then fill.

If using a top crust, roll remaining dough large enough to cover pie, and place on top of pie. Cut slits near center, or use a small cookie cutter to cut out a shape. The cut out piece may be overlaid beside the hole in the crust if desired; just be sure to leave a little space uncovered for venting. Seal crusts by folding edge of top crust under the edge of the bottom crust and pressing, or by crimping with fork or pinching with fingers. Trim excess dough from around edge of pie pan.

Combine remaining 1/2 egg with milk and spread over top crust, then sprinkle with sugar before baking.

The edge crust of a pie will often begin to burn before the pie is done. To prevent this, fold a piece of aluminum foil around the edge of the crust. Some people do this partway through baking, but I tend to burn myself doing it that way, so I start baking with the foil around it, and remove the foil about half way through.

PUMPION PYE (OLDE ENGLISH PUMPKIN PIE)

This recipe for "Pumpion Pye" is from the cookbook *The Compleat Cook*, printed in London in 1671. Original spelling and punctuation preserved.

Take about half a pound of Pumpion and slice it, a handfull of tyme, a little rosemary, parsley and sweet marjorum slipped off the stalks, and chop them small, then take the cynamon, nutmeg, pepper and six cloves, and beat them, take ten eggs and beat them, then mix them and beat them all together and put in as much sugar as you think fit, then fry them like a froize*, after it is fryed, let it stand till it be cold, then fill your pye, take sliced apples thinne round wayes, and lay a rowe of the froize, and layer the apples with currents betwixt the layer while your pye is fitted, and put in a good deal of sweet Butter before you close it, when pye is baked, take six yelks of eggs, some whitewine or vergis*, and make a caudle* of this, but not too thick, cut up the lid and put it in, stir them well together whilst the eggs and pumpions be not perceived and so serve it up.

*froize: a kind of pancake
*vergis: juice from crab apples, unripened grapes, or other sour fruit
*caudle: a warm spiced and sugared drink

DEEP AND RICH PUMPKIN PIE

This is a more modern version of the traditional Thanksgiving pie.

(Note: if you're going to décorate with sugared cranberries, be sure to start them the night before. Recipe on page 43.)

Pastry crust
2 cups pumpkin puree (you can buy this or cook and mash a pie pumpkin)
3 large eggs
1- 1/4 cups packed brown sugar
1 tablespoon cornstarch
1/2 teaspoon salt
1- 1/2 teaspoons ground cinnamon
1/2 teaspoon ground ginger
1/4 teaspoon ground nutmeg
1/8 teaspoon ground cloves
1 cup heavy cream
1/4 cup milk

Preheat oven to 375°. Pre-bake the crust for 5 - 10 minutes.

Whisk the pumpkin, 3 eggs, and brown sugar together until combined. Add the cornstarch, salt, cinnamon, ginger, nutmeg, cloves, cream, and milk. Vigorously whisk until everything is combined. Filling will be a little thick.

Pour filling into the pre-baked crust. Bake one hour or until the center is almost set. (The center may still quiver, but the rest should be set.) Cool completely.

Note: The filling can be made up to a month ahead of time and kept in a plastic bag in the freezer. Remove from freezer and place in refrigerator the night before using to thaw.

Or, it can be made the night before and kept in the refrigerator overnight.

Décorate pie with sugared cranberries if desired. Keep in refrigerator.

NANNY'S CANTALOUPE PIE

This recipe has been in my husband's family for generations, and I know of at least 3 people (including myself) who have won blue ribbons at county fairs with it. It's my husband's favorite dessert.

Preheat oven to 350° and prebake the pie crust for 10 minutes.

Peel, de-seed, and chop one large, ripe cantaloupe. Put in a pot with 1 cup sugar and cook over low heat until cantaloupe is translucent, stirring as needed. (Do not add water or anything else; the cantaloupe will juice out, and as the sugar melts it will provide its own liquid.)

Mash the cantaloupe. Stir in 3 beaten eggs, 1 cup milk, and one cup diced pineapple.

Pour into pie pan lined with pre-baked crust and bake about 50 minutes, until lightly golden on top and still a little bit quivery in the middle; it will set up more as it cools. Do not cut until completely cool. Serve with real whipped cream, if desired.

This recipe is for a large pie. I use a 10" pie plate. Some of the relatives use a deep 8", you must be careful not to burn the bottom before the pie cooks through if you do that.

The pineapple is the secret ingredient. I've seen other cantaloupe pie recipes, but none with pineapple, and it really does set off the cantaloupe nicely. I admit to using a small can of crushed pineapple tidbits instead of fresh pineapple; just be sure it's drained.

Let them give thanks to the Lord for His unfailing love and His wonderful deeds for men. ~Psalm 107:8

MIMI'S APPLE PIE

I've won blue ribbons with this apple pie recipe of my mother's. It's a no-fail recipe that gets raves every time.

6 apples, peeled, cored and sliced
1 tablespoon lemon juice
1 cup sugar
1/2 cup old-fashioned rolled oats (not instant or thick cut or steel cut)
1 egg
sprinkle of salt
2 teaspoons cinnamon
1/2 teaspoon nutmeg
About 1/3 stick butter
Top and bottom pie crusts
Optional:
1 cup pecans or walnuts (these aren't optional if my husband will be eating it)
3/4 cup raisins or sugared cranberries (recipe on page 43)

Preheat oven to 350° and prebake bottom pie crust.

Mix all ingredients (except crusts) together; pour into pie pan lined with crust. Dot generously with butter. Top with second crust; crimp edges and cut vents in top.

For a shiny, flaky top crust, baste it with a mixture of egg and milk; then sprinkle sugar over it. Bake at 350° for one hour.

SOUTHERN PECAN PIE

This is the classic.

1 pie crust
1 cup corn syrup - light or dark
3 eggs
1 cup sugar
2 tablespoons butter, melted
1 teaspoon vanilla extract
1-1/2 cups pecans

Preheat oven to 350°. Prebake pie crust for 5 – 10 minutes.

Mix corn syrup, eggs, sugar, butter, and vanilla using a spoon. Stir in pecans. Pour filling into pie crust.

Bake on center rack of oven for 60 to 70 minutes. Cool for 2 hours on wire rack before serving.

To use frozen pie crust: Place cookie sheet in oven and preheat oven as directed. Pour filling into frozen crust and bake on preheated cookie sheet.

To tell when pie is done, tap the center surface lightly - it should spring back when done.

MIMI'S CHESS PIE

This makes Thanksgiving; I'd as soon skip the turkey and dressing as this pie.
Chess pie is a custard pie flavored with nutmeg; it reminds me of baked eggnog.
This is another blue-ribbon pie everyone loves.

1 pie crust
3 eggs
1- 3/4 cups sugar
1/2 cup melted butter
1- 1/2 tablespoons flour
1/2 cup + 1 tablespoon cream
1- 1/2 teaspoons vanilla
3/4 teaspoon nutmeg

Preheat oven to 450°. Prebake pie crust for 5 – 10 minutes.

Cream together eggs and sugar. Stir in butter, then whisk in flour, then cream.
Stir in vanilla and nutmeg.

Pour mixture into prebaked pie crust and bake at 450° for 10 minutes; then
reduce heat to 300° and bake another 45 minutes, or until set and golden
brown on top.

GRANNY LIL'S LEMON MERINGUE PIE

For a lighter taste on Thanksgiving, try this real lemon pie from my father's family. It's another blue ribbon winner.

1/2 cup + 1 tablespoon cornstarch
2 cups sugar, divided
A pinch of salt (about half of a 1/4 teaspoon)
1- 3/4 cups hot water
4 eggs, separated
1- 1/2 tablespoons butter
2 teaspoons fresh lemon zest
1/2 cup freshly-squeezed lemon juice
10" prebaked pie crust
1/4 teaspoon cream of tartar

Preheat oven to 450°. Prebake pie crust for 10 minutes.

Combine cornstarch, 1- 1/2 cups of sugar, and salt in a medium saucepan. Gradually whisk in hot water; mix well. Cook over medium heat, stirring constantly, until thick and bubbly. Lower heat and cook 1 minute.

In a medium bowl, beat egg yolks. Stir in 1/2 cup of the hot mixture from the stove, then stir back into the saucepan. Cook 2 minutes, stirring constantly. Remove from heat; stir in butter and lemon zest. Gradually stir in lemon juice. Cool 5 minutes, then pour into pie pan lined with prebaked pie crust.

Beat egg whites with a dash of salt until foamy. Add cream of tartar; beat until soft peaks form. Slowly beat in remaining 1/2 cup sugar, a tablespoon at a time, until stiff peaks form. Spoon over filling.

Brown on middle rack in oven for 5 minutes. Allow to cool completely, and keep in refrigerator.

KAY'S BROWNIES

Some people don't like pie, so it's nice to have a couple of different options for dessert. These brownies will please any chocolate lovers.

4 squares unsweetened baking chocolate
3/4 cup butter
2 cups sugar
3 eggs
1 teaspoon vanilla
1 cup flour
1 cup chopped pecans

Preheat oven to 350° (325° if using a glass baking dish).

Melt chocolate and butter together in double boiler (or microwave on high for 2 minutes) and mix well.

Stir sugar into chocolate until well blended. Mix in eggs and vanilla, then flour and pecans, until well blended.

Spread into buttered 9" x 13" baking pan and bake about 30 minutes, or just until toothpick inserted in center comes out with fudgey crumbs. Do not over-bake. Cool completely in pan and cut into squares.

PAWPAW'S BANANA PUDDING

Another from Granny Lil, this is Pawpaw's favorite dessert. Boxes of pudding weren't allowed in our house.

3/4 cup sugar
4 tablespoons cornstarch
1/4 teaspoon salt
4 egg yolks
1/2 cup milk
2- 1/2 cups half & half
4 tablespoons butter
1- 1/2 teaspoons vanilla
Bananas
Vanilla wafer cookies

Combine sugar, cornstarch, and salt in top of double boiler. Beat in egg yolks and milk.

Add half & half while cooking in double boiler and cook until thick.

Remove from heat and stir in butter and vanilla.

Layer cookies and bananas in a bowl. Pour pudding over them. Repeat layers until you run out of pudding. Top with cookies and bananas.

LEFTOVERS

With such a feast, there are bound to be leftovers. Following are some recipes to use them up in creative and delicious ways.

STIR-FRIED TURKEY RICE

Cook 1 cup rice per instructions on package.

When done, place in wok or heavy skillet in 2 tablespoons canola oil. Stir in 2 cup chopped turkey, 1 chopped onion, 1/4 cup hoisin sauce, and 1 cup chicken stock. Cook, stirring frequently, until liquid is reduced.

Stir in 1 cup cranberries. Any other leftover vegetables may also be added if desired.

Serve hot.

CRANBERRY TURNOVERS

Preheat oven to 350°.

Blend 8 oz. soft cream cheese with 2 cups confectioner's sugar. Set aside.

Unroll crescent rolls or puff pastry (or, if you have extra unbaked pie crust, it can be used).

Drop a tablespoon of cream cheese mixture and 2 tablespoons cranberry sauce in center of each.

Roll or fold into mini turnovers. Bake for 15 minutes.

If desired, make a frosting with confectioner's sugar thinned with water.

Keep your eyes open to your mercies. The man who forgets to be thankful has fallen asleep in life.
~Robert Louis Stevenson

TURKEY JOES

Chop 2 cups turkey fine. Set aside.

Sauté one onion in butter until soft.

Stir in 1 can tomato paste, 2 tablespoons chili powder, 1 teaspoon dry ground mustard, 1/2 teaspoon paprika, 1/2 teaspoon salt. Stir while cooking about 3 minutes.

Stir in 1 can chicken broth, 1/3 cup ketchup, 1/4 cup Worcestershire sauce and chopped turkey.

Reduce heat to medium, cover, simmer 25 minutes.

Serve on sweet potato biscuits.

SWEET POTATO BISCUITS

Preheat oven to 475°.

Mix 3 cups flour, 1- 1/2 tablespoons baking powder, 1- 1/2 teaspoons salt, and 1 tablespoon sugar. Cut in 1/2 cup chilled firm butter.

Stir 1-1/2 cups cold cooked sweet potatoes with 2 tablespoons buttermilk. Stir potato mixture into flour mixture until dough forms.

Form into 3/4" thick circle. Cut out biscuits. Place on lightly greased baking pan and place on top oven rack. Bake 15-20 minutes.

Very good with fried eggs & pan-fried turkey, or as a bun for Turkey Joes.

THANKSGIVING SHEPHERD'S PIE

Preheat oven to 400°.

Press dressing into a pie plate or casserole dish. Fill with chopped turkey and any leftover vegetables – green beans, peas, squash, corn, etc.

Dot with butter. Top with mashed potatoes. Bake until heated through and golden brown on top, about 25 minutes.

THANKSGIVING FRITTATA

Preheat oven to 300°.

Whisk 6 eggs, 1 cup half and half, 1 teaspoon salt, 1/2 teaspoon pepper. Heat 2 cups sweet potatoes in 1 tablespoon butter over medium heat.

Set aside; sauté 2 cups sprouts and kale salad until tender.

Stir into potatoes.

Pour into greased casserole; pour egg mixture over.

Sprinkle with 1/2 cup cheese.

Bake 12 minutes or until set.

POTATO PANCAKES

Sauté 1 small onion in butter.

Slowly sprinkle 1 cup flour into hot butter, stirring all the while.

Stir into 2 cups mashed potatoes.

Add 2 teaspoons rosemary and 1/2 teaspoon powdered garlic. Stir well. Form into pancakes and pan fry in butter until warmed through.

Salt and pepper to taste.

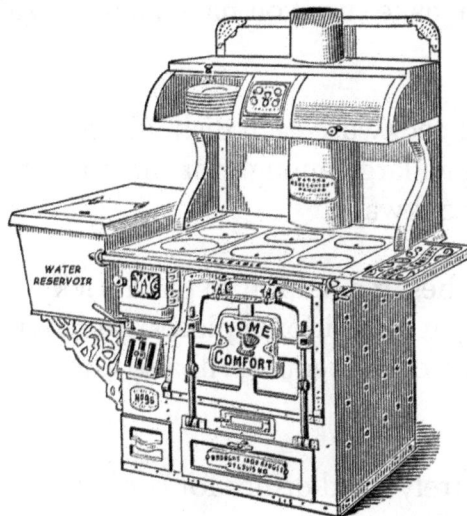

TIMELINE

- Cucumbers and squash are plentiful in the summer. If you want to have homemade Granny's Salad Pickles and Nanny's Sunshine Relish at Thanksgiving, August is a good month to make them.

- Parched corn can also be made months ahead of time.

As early as the first week in November:

- Create a guest list and send invitations. Remember to ask about any dietary restrictions/allergies so you can plan the menu accordingly.

- If ordering a turkey, do it now. Rule of thumb: order a pound per person.

- Schedule any carpet cleaning or other cleaning, maintenance, or yard work. These companies will get very busy as the holiday approaches, so it's best to get on the list early.

- You can mix the pastry for pie crusts and the dough for angel biscuits (or any type of bread) up to three months ahead of time and keep it in the freezer. If you do this, put pie crusts and un-formed biscuit dough in the refrigerator to thaw the day before you want to use them; bake already-cut biscuits frozen.

- Check your linens to make sure you have plenty. Wash them or have them cleaned if necessary.

- Decide what piece of cookware each dish will be prepared in. Make sure you have a roasting pan large enough for the bird. If necessary, purchase or borrow any needed cookware.

- Plan your serving dishes. It's helpful to put a sticky note on each piece. Not only will this show you if additional pieces are required, but if you have help on Thanksgiving, other people will also know which dishes to use for which food.

- If you're using any rarely-used dishes for cooking, serving, or on the table, check to see if any dust has accumulated in storage and clean if necessary.

- Plan your tableware. Polish the silver if necessary. Wipe crystal to remove any fingerprints.

- There will likely be several dishes of leftovers after the meal. If plasticware or other storage containers will be needed for them, they can be purchased now. You may also want to get a few foil plates for guests to take some leftovers home with them.

- Plan the table centerpiece and other décor, and gather needed items (except fresh flowers). Get as much decorating done as you can early in the month.

The second week of November:

- If making homemade stock, now is the time to visit your local butcher or grocery meat department for some turkey necks and other inexpensive pieces to use for the stock. The stock can be made now and frozen. Remove from freezer and place in refrigerator to thaw the day before it will be needed.

- Once you have stock, you can also make the gravy and freeze it. Again, remove it from the freezer the day before Thanksgiving to thaw.

- Finalize the menu. Gather recipes for each dish, and make a list of required ingredients. Check off what you have, then make separate lists of needed perishables and nonperishables. Nonperishable items can be purchased now, before stock gets low in the stores.

- Plan seating. You don't have to assign seating, although you can, but be sure you will have enough table space and plenty of chairs for everyone to sit down and enjoy the meal.

- Plan games, crafts, and activities and obtain any needed items.

- Make a music playlist and copies of readings if needed. For both music and readings, be sure to have a variety of styles to please various tastes. Decide if you'll need another table and/or chairs for the activities, since the dinner table will already be set.

Third week of November:

- Clean house, especially the parts that will be open to guests. If you'll be hosting overnight guests, be sure there are fresh linens on the bed and in the bathroom.

- The filling for any custard pie (such as pumpkin or chess pie) can be made now and frozen, unbaked. Thaw before baking.

- Cornbread for the dressing can also be made now and frozen. Remove from freezer and wrap in a clean, dry towel to thaw the day before using.

- Purchase heavy cream, whipping cream, and half-and-half needed for any recipes. These are usually hard to find just before Thanksgiving.

The weekend before Thanksgiving:

- If you have a frozen bird, remove it from the freezer in plenty of time to thaw out by Thanksgiving. Rule of thumb: allow 24 hours for each 4 pounds of bird.

Monday before Thanksgiving:

- Purchase perishables.

- If alcohol will be served, plan a bar area near the dining area. If needed, obtain a cooler to hold beverages so your refrigerator will be free for foodstuffs.

- If serving pinto beans, they can be cooked today.

- If sugared cranberries will be used in any recipe (or for snacking) they can be made today (see page 43).

Tuesday before Thanksgiving:

- If you made any pie crust, bread dough, cornbread, stock, or gravy ahead of time, take it out of the freezer to thaw.

Let us be grateful to the people who make us happy; they are the charming gardeners who make our souls blossom. ~Marcel Proust

- Make the cranberry sauce.

- Make onion rings for green bean casserole if required.

- Purchase fresh flowers for the centerpiece or any other décor items. Put up any remaining décor needed.

- If you have freezer room and haven't done so before now, you can make the rolls (or biscuits or bread) and keep them in the freezer until ready to bake on Thanksgiving Day.

- If you don't have an automatic ice maker, either purchase bags of ice or begin freezing ice now.

The day before Thanksgiving:

- Make a detailed checklist of what you have to do tomorrow. Note how long each task will take to complete, and plan your day accordingly. Write down what time to begin each task.

- Bake pies.

- Boil eggs, and wash, peel, and chop onions, celery, and any other vegetables (except for any salad items). Cover potatoes with water to prevent browning. Do the same for the sweet potatoes. Keep all vegetables and eggs in refrigerator overnight.

- Brine turkey if desired.

- If serving stuffed squash, you can make it today and keep, wrapped, in refrigerator overnight.

- Bake cornbread for the dressing if it wasn't done ahead of time.

- Cook green beans if serving them or using them in green bean casserole.

- Chill wine. Prepare cooler for drinks if necessary.

- Set the table.

- Set out any items needed for games, crafts, or activities.

Thanksgiving Day:

- Assign someone to be in charge of the music, and someone to watch over activities of children, if necessary.

- If roasting a turkey, start it according to the plan you made yesterday.

- While the turkey is roasting, mix any beverages.

- Mix the dressing and green bean casserole. Keep in refrigerator until ready to bake.

- About a half hour before the turkey is done, put the potatoes and sweet potatoes on to boil. When the potatoes are soft, prepare them according to recipe and keep warm on back burner or in slow cooker.

- When the turkey is done, let it sit while you heat all other hot dishes. First, put the dressing in to bake. After about 15 minutes, put the green bean casserole in.

- Prepare and salads or other fresh dishes.

- Place a few grains of parched corn at each plate if desired.

- Bake the angel biscuits.

- Add marshmallows to sweet potatoes and brown, if necessary.

- Add fried onions and/or cheese to top of green bean casserole, if necessary.

- Make the gravy.

- Enjoy!

Décor

Appropriate décorations will reflect the bounty of the season; cornucopias (also called horns of plenty) are perfect. A cornucopia is a type of basket or container shaped like a hollowed-out cone and slightly bent like a horn.

To make miniature cornucopias, use sugar cones. Dip the bottom third into hot water for 20 seconds, then place in the microwave for 20 seconds. While still warm, bend slightly. As the cone cools, it will harden in shape. Fill these mini horns with nuts, berries, small candies, little squares of cheese and sausage with goldfish crackers – anything that will fit. They can be used as hors d'oeuvres or snacks, or placed at each setting at the table with a name card attached to assign seating.

For a larger cornucopia, use a large water bottle as a mold. Preheat the oven to 400°. Meanwhile, crush the top of the water bottle a bit so that it is more cone shaped. Fold a large square of aluminum foil in half to form a rectangle. Wrap loosely around the bottle, starting at the top of the bottle, which will be the tail of the horn. If necessary, use more foil to make sure there are no gaps. Remove the water bottle and bend the foil slightly, adjusting to the shape of a cornucopia. Stuff with more foil to hold its shape. Spray the foil horn lightly with cooking oil.

Roll out a can of crescent rolls, pizza dough, or breadsticks to a thin rectangle, about 1/4" thick. Cut into strips 1" wide. Starting at the tail, wrap the dough strips around the cornucopia, slightly overlapping and pressing seams together. You may need to slightly moisten the dough with water for them to stick. When the entire foil horn is wrapped, bake for about 45 minutes. When done, remove from oven and allow to cool. Remove the foil carefully. Spray the cornucopia all over, inside and out, with cooking oil. This will seal the bread, so it won't absorb moisture and go limp. Fill with fruit or anything you wish.

Another pretty way to display a symbol of harvest is with a large pumpkin. Choose one that is slightly flat on top and bottom. Cut the top off flat – you'll want a much larger opening than for a jack-o'-lantern. Remove the insides. Spray well with shellac inside and out to prevent rotting. Let dry completely before proceeding.

The pumpkin may be filled with a flower arrangement, a tall candle, pine cones, or fruit and vegetables. If putting edibles in the pumpkin, place waxed paper between the shellaced pumpkin and the foodstuff.

For smaller areas, place a candle inside a large jar, and surround with a variety of unshelled nuts in the bottom few inches of the vase. Dried corn or popcorn kernels could also be used.

Make a wreath for the front door with a few simple materials. Shape a circle of the size you want from wire hanger or floral wire. Crumple old newspaper and twist around the hanger for padding. Cover with a couple layers of burlap so you can't see the newspaper through it. Using pins or hot-glue, attach many artificial leaves in various fall colors. Over the leaves, attach miniature pinecones, ears of Indian corn, heads of wheat, and/or other symbols of the season. Tie jute or raffia on top, keeping one end free. Tie the free end into a loop to use as a hanger.

Because Thanksgiving is rooted in the generosity of the Wampanoag (who were a tribe of the Iroquois), you may want to incorporate some symbols from the Iroquois Confederation into your décorations. Their symbols are:

- A cluster of five arrows: unity. If the nations of the Confederacy remain joined together, they cannot be broken.

- White pine tree: Tree of Peace. The tribes of the Iroquois at one time fought with one another, but the people grew tired of the fighting. So they agreed to bury their weapons under a giant white pine tree. The white pine tree is a symbol of the unity of the nations. Its needles, which always grow in clusters of five, are symbolic of the uniting of the nations. The white pine also has broad branches that can provide shelter for the Iroquois peoples.

- Four white roots: the cardinal points. The four white roots at the base of the Great Tree of Peace represent the points north, south, east and west. By following these roots, all nations can find the Great Tree of Peace.

- Eagle: protector. The eagle is the protector of peace. Perched atop the Tree of Peace, it alerts the people if danger approaches.

- Long house: harmony. Within a long house, families all live together in harmony. With the nations united, they are all one family living territorially in one long house.

- Circle: strength and the cycles of life. If the people remain united in a circle, they can surround the Tree of Peace and keep it standing; but if they let go of each other and break the circle, the Tree could fall to the ground. Then so too would the peace.

- Semi-circle: the sky world. A pattern of a semi-circles is often seen in many beaded designs or quill work, and represents a huge overhead dome to recognize the Sky World, from where life came.

- Turtle: earth. The turtle is a symbol for the earth, as it is said that the turtle carries Earth on its back. In the creation story, it was the turtle who carried sky woman on his back.

77

Fall leaves, pine trees and pines cones, turkeys, corn, and gourds are all suitable for Thanksgiving décorations. Squirrels, who gather nuts in fall for the coming winter, are a fitting symbol. Your imagination is the only limit.

Scents can help create ambiance. Place the peel of an orange and a cinnamon stick into a saucepot and just cover with water; simmer on the back of the stove to create a natural Thanksgiving aroma. A couple of drops of vanilla extract could also be included. For a spicier scent, add a few cloves. If you don't wish to have the stove on, squirt a few drops of your favorite essential oil fragrance onto a light bulb. You can also purchase scented candles.

TURKEY-FOLDED NAPKINS

Fold your napkin into a rectangle, matching the edges carefully, with the short edges towards you and the long folded edge to your right.

Pick up both edges of one of the closest short, folded sides. Fold this edge over and under in accordion-style pleats about one inch wide. Continue forming these pleats until you have reached about three-quarters of the way across your napkin rectangle. For extra hold, you may want to spray and re-iron each pleat. If not, be sure to finger-press each pleat edge. End with all your pleats on top of your last folded pleat, and on top of the remaining flat fabric.

Place both thumbs under the fabric pleats in the center of their width and rest your hands on top of your pleats. Fold the left side under the right side and place on your working surface carefully.

Above the folded pleats, will be your un-pleated section of cloth. Pick up the far right corner which will have four layers of cloth in it, and bring in down toward the near left corner of the flat cloth section, creating a triangle. Tuck under, finger-press or iron this fold.

Lift up your napkin and place the open pleat edges upwards, and the long section of your triangle downwards. Allow the pleats to fan out towards your working surface, creating the tail of your cloth napkin turkey.

Giving Thanks

The giving of thanks is the intent of the day, and some time should be set aside for that purpose. The best way to give thanks is from the heart, but for a little inspiration, some prayers and toasts are given below, followed by historic proclamations, poems, and stories about gratitude.

The following prayers, meditations, and blessings have been gathered from many cultures. Just as the Native Americans and the Puritans gave thanks in their own ways, so today many peoples have differing ways of expressing gratitude. Realizing that people of different regions and religions also give thanks for their blessings can help us focus on things we all have in common, and promote peace and harmony among all peoples and cultures. That would surely be something to be thankful for.

PRAYERS, MEDITATIONS, AND BLESSINGS

O Lord our God and heavenly Father, which of Thy unspeakable mercy towards us, hast provided meate and drinke for the nourishment of our weake bodies. Grant us peace to use them reverently, as from Thy hands, with thankful hearts: let Thy blessing rest upon these Thy good creatures, to our comfort and sustentation: and grant we humbly beseech Thee, good Lord, that as we doe hunger and thirst for this food of our bodies, so our soules may earnestly long after the food of eternal life, through Jesus Christ, our Lord and Saviour, Amen.
~George Webb, 1625 (original spelling preserved)

Blessed art Thou, O Lord our God, King of the Universe,
Who creates all living beings and the things they need.
For all that Thou hast created to sustain the life of every living being,
blessed be Thou, the Life of the universe.
~Jewish prayer

Father of us all,
This meal is a sign of Your love for us:
Bless us and bless our food,
And help us to give You glory each day
Through Jesus Christ our Lord, Amen.
~Catholic Grace Prayer

This ritual is one.
The food is one.
We who offer the food are one.
The fire of hunger is also one.
All action is one.
We who understand this are one.
~Hindu prayer for meals

1 Make a joyful noise unto the Lord, all ye lands.
2 Serve the Lord with gladness: come before His presence with singing.
3 Know ye that the Lord He is God: it is He that hath made us, and not we ourselves; we are His people, and the sheep of His pasture.
4 Enter into His gates with thanksgiving, and into His courts with praise: be thankful unto Him, and bless His name.
5 For the Lord is good; His mercy is everlasting; and His truth endureth to all generations.
~Psalm 100

This food is the gift of the whole universe—the earth, the sky, and much hard work.
May we live in a way that makes us worthy to receive it.
May we transform our unskillful states of mind, especially our greed.
May we take only foods that nourish us and prevent illness.
We accept this food so that we may realize the path of practice.
~Thich Nhat Hanh

Come, Lord Jesus, our guest to be
And bless these gifts bestowed by Thee.
And bless our loved ones everywhere,
And keep them in Your loving care.
~Moravian Blessing

80

GIVING THANKS

Toward the east:
From the appearing way, Merciful Creator, thank You for the sun which purifies. It brings light into the world, enlightenment into the darkness, and understanding to the ignorant. Help us to be the bearers of Your light.

Toward the north:
From the way of the cold, Great Creator, thank You for the cold, the snow that winter brings. It brings purity to the earth and renews Your creation. Thank You for the seasons of winter in our lives. It is our facing of such trials that allows You to renew our lives. Grant us the strength to endure.

Toward the west:
From the disappearing way, Father, thank You for the stories, the experiences, the stories of Your faithfulness to Your people. Grant us the ears to listen and to hear You, and the wisdom to live accordingly.

Toward the south:
From the way of the warm, Creator of life, thank You for the times of growth we experience. Thank You for nurturing us and helping us grow. Enable us to help others.

Down:
From the way of the low, Creator of Earth, we give You thanks for providing our every need, for calling us out of the Earth and seeking a relationship with us, and granting us the opportunity to be in sacred relationship with You and all of Your creation.

In:
From the center of our being, Creator of within, we pray in all of these directions, remembering Your faithfulness, and with all of who we are, we offer ourselves and our prayers to You this day.

Up:
From the uppermost way, Creator of the highest, Wi hi yo Ya wi hi ya We he yah Ya wi hi yu.
~Cherokee Prayer of Thanksgiving

God, the Father & Son of the land, of the waters, of the rivers,
Make a path for us to gather!
If we listen to the land, to God,
To our old men and women of the Dreaming,
They will say 'Come here to this country, and you will feel well!'
If we listen, we will understand.
~Australian Aboriginal prayer

Our praise to You, Lord our God and King of all, for giving us life, sustaining us, and enabling us to reach this season.
~Jewish prayer

O God, when I have food, help me to remember the hungry;
When I have work, help me to remember the jobless;
When I have a home, help me remember those who have no home;
When I am without pain, help me to remember those who suffer,
And remembering, help me to destroy my complacency;
Bestir my compassion, and be concerned enough to help
By word and deed, those who cry out for what we take for granted.
Amen.
~Samuel F. Pugh

How can we render Thee thanks, O Lord? Thy bounties are endless and our gratitude cannot equal them. How can the finite utter praise of the infinite? Unable are we to voice our thanks for Thy favors, and in utter powerlessness we turn wholly to Thy kingdom, beseeching the increase of Thy bestowals and bounties. Thou art the Giver, the Bestower, the Almighty.
~Baha'i prayer by Abdu'l-Bahá

GIVING THANKS

O Lord, since we have feasted thus,
Which we so little merit,
Let Meg now take away the flesh,
And Jock bring in the spirit!
~Robert Burns, A Grace After Dinner

We return thanks to our mother, the earth, which sustains us with all things.
We return thanks to the rivers and streams, which supply us with water.
We return thanks to all herbs, which furnish medicines for the cure of our
sicknesses. We return thanks to the sun, which has looked upon the earth with
a beneficent eye to give us warmth. We return thanks to the moon and stars,
which have given to us their light when the sun is gone. Lastly, we return
thanks to the Great Spirit, in Whom is embodied all goodness, and Who directs
all things for the good of His children.
~Haudenosaunee (Iroquois) Thanksgiving Prayer

With bended knees, with hands outstretched, do I yearn for the effective
expression of the Holy Spirit working within me:
For this love and understanding, truth and justice;
for wisdom to know the apparent from the real, that I might alleviate the
sufferings of men on earth.
God is love, understanding, wisdom, and virtue.
Let us love one another, let us practice mercy and forgiveness, let us have
peace, born of fellow-feeling.
Let my joy be of altruistic living, of doing good to others. Happiness is unto
him from whom happiness proceeds to any other human being.
~Zoroastrian Prayer

O Lord, when hunger pinches sore,
Do Thou stand us in stead,
And send us, from Thy bounteous store,
A tup or wether head! Amen.
~Robert Burns

So remember Me; I will remember you.
And be grateful to Me and do not deny Me.
~Qur'an 2:152

Give thanks, all ye people, give thanks to the Lord,
Alleluias of freedom with joyful accord:
Let the East and the West, North and South roll along,
Sea, mountain, and prairie, one thanksgiving song.
~From The President's Hymn written by William Augustus Muhlenburg for
President Abraham Lincoln, 1863

When Serving Food:
In this food I see clearly the presence of the entire universe supporting my
existence.
Looking at the Filled Plate:
All living beings are struggling for life. May they all have enough food to eat
today.
Just Before Eating:
The plate is filled with food. I am aware that each morsel is the fruit of much
hard work by those who produced it.
Beginning to Eat:
With the first taste, I promise to practice loving kindness. With the second,
I promise to relieve the suffering of others. With the third, I promise to see
others' joy as my own. With the fourth, I promise to learn the way of non-
attachment and equanimity.
Finishing the Meal:
The plate is empty. My hunger is satisfied. I vow to live for the benefit of all
beings.
~Buddhist Prayer Ceremony from Thich Nhat Hanh

Gratitude may be in the heart, in submission and humility; on the tongue,
in praise and acknowledgment; and in the physical faculties, by means of
obedience and submission.
~Ibn al-Qayyim

O Lord, How full is this world of Your unending creativity.
How astounding is creation in all its variety.
How breathtaking is new life, growth and transformation.
How wonderful is Your provision for us, Your children!
This day, we celebrate Your great goodness with thankful hearts and joyful
lives. Amen.
~Unknown

If the only prayer you ever say in your life is "thank you," it will be enough. ~Meister Eckhart

GIVING THANKS

And (remember) when your Lord proclaimed: 'If you give thanks, I will give you more of My blessings; but if you are thankless, verily, My punishment is indeed severe.'
~Qur'an 14:7

O Creator of our land, our earth, the trees,
the animals and humans, all is for Your honor.
The drums beat it out, and people sing about it,
and they dance with noisy joy that You are the Lord.
You also have pulled the other continents out of the sea.
What a wonderful world You have made out of the wet mud,
and what beautiful men and women!
We thank You for the beauty of this earth.
The grace of Your creation is like a cool day between rainy seasons.
We drink in Your creation with our eyes.
We listen to the birds' jubilee with our ears.
How strong and good Your earth smells, and everything that grows there.
The sky above us is like a warm, soft Kente cloth, because You are behind it,
else it would be cold and rough and uncomfortable.
We drink in Your creation and cannot get enough of it.
~African prayer of thanksgiving

Now that I am about to eat, O Great Spirit, give my thanks to the beasts and birds whom You have provided for my hunger; and pray deliver my sorrow that living things must make a sacrifice for my comfort and well-being. Let the feather of corn spring up in its time, and let it not wither but make full grains for the fires of our cooking pots, now that I am about to eat.
~Native American prayer

Let us together be protected and nourished by God's blessings. Let us together join our mental forces in strength for the benefit of humanity. Let our efforts at learning be luminous and filled with joy, and endowed with purpose. Let there be peace and serenity in all the three universes.
~A Hindu prayer from the Holy Upanishads

Blessed are You, LORD our God, King of the universe, Who brings forth bread from the earth.
~Traditional Jewish blessing

King of heaven, You have revealed Your wonder even to someone as vile as me.

You have taken from me the false joy of earthly pleasures, and given me instead the true joy of Your heavenly love.

You have taken me into Your heavenly family, treating me as a beloved child. And I cling to You as a small child clings to its mother.

I will never let go; I will always stay in Your presence.

King of heaven, You have showered Your wealth even onto someone as undeserving as me.

You have taken from me any desire for the perishable riches of earth, and given me instead only the desire for the imperishable wealth of heaven.

You have taken me into Your royal court, treating me as the chief steward of Your spiritual treasures.

I bow before You as a servant bows to his master.

I will never cease to adore You; I will always strive to serve You.

~Tamil (Sri Lankan) prayer by Manikka Vasahar

O Thou who kindly dost provide for every creature's want,
We bless the God of Nature wide, for all Thy goodness lent.
And if it please Thee, heavenly Guide, may never worse be sent;
But, whether granted or denied, Lord, bless us with content.
~A Grace Before Dinner 1, Robert Burns

May the Great Architect of the universe bless that which His bounty has prepared for us, and may He give us grateful hearts and help us to supply the wants and needs of our fellow creatures. So mote it be.
~A Masonic grace

Some hae meat and canna eat,
And some wad eat that want it;
But we hae meat, and we can eat,
Sae let the Lord be thankit.
~Galloway/Selkirk Grace (often wrongly attributed to Robert Burns)

May the Lord accept this, our offering, and bless our food that it may bring us strength in our body, vigor in our mind, and selfless devotion in our hearts for His service.
~Vedanta prayer by Swami Paramananda

GIVING THANKS

Oh Lord that lends me life, lend me a heart replete with thankfulness.
~William Shakespeare

Oh Allah! Whatever blessings I or any of Your creatures rose up with, is only from You. You have no partner, so all grace and thanks are due to You.
~Du'a from the Sunnah (prayer from the oral teaching of Islamic tradition)

O God, we thank Thee for this universe, our great home; for its vastness and its riches, and for the manifoldness of the life which teems upon it and of which we are part.
We praise Thee for the arching sky and the blessed winds, for the driving clouds and the constellations on high.
We praise Thee for the salt sea and the running water, for the everlasting hills, for the trees, and for the grass under our feet.
We thank Thee for our senses by which we can see the splendor of the morning, and hear the jubilant songs of love, and smell the breath of the springtime.
Grant us, we pray Thee, a heart open to all this joy and beauty, and save our souls from being so steeped in care or so darkened by passion that we pass heedless and unseeing when even the thorn-bush by the wayside is aflame with the glory of God.
~ Walter Rauschenbusch, Baptist Minister

You, O God, are the Lord of the mountains and valleys. You are my mother and my father.

You have given rain to make the corn grow, and sunshine to ripen it. Now in Your strength the harvest begins.

I offer You the first morsels of the harvest. I know it is small compared with the abundance of the crop. But since You have provided the harvest, my gift to You is only a sign of what You have given to me.

You alone know how many suns and moons it will take to finish reaping. You alone know how heavy the crop will be. If I work too hard and too fast, I forget about You, Who gave me the harvest. So I will work steadily and slowly, remembering that each ear of corn is a priceless gift from You.

~Sioux harvest prayer

Countless are Your names, countless Your dwelling-places;
The breadth of Your kingdom is beyond our imagination.
Even to try and imagine Your kingdom is foolish.
Yet through words and through music
We speak Your name and sing Your praise.
Words are the only tools we have to proclaim Your greatness,
And music our only means of echoing Your virtue.
You put words in our hearts and minds.
With words we can describe the glory of Your creation,
And so our words can reflect Your glory.
You put music in our hearts and minds.
With music we can echo the beauty of heaven,
And so our music can express our deepest wish.
How can someone as insignificant as me
Express the vastness and wonder of Your creation?
How can someone as sinful as me
Dare to hope for a place in heaven?
My only answer lies in the words and the music
Which You Yourself have given me.

~Sikh Prayer by Guru Nanak

Itadakimasu ("I receive the lives of animals and plants for my own life.")
Gochisousama ("It was a feast which entertained and provided hospitality to me.")

~Japanese expressions before and after a meal

88

GIVING THANKS

The eyes of all wait upon Thee; and Thou givest them their meat in due season.
Thou openest Thine hand, and satisfiest the desire of every living thing.
~Russian Orthodox grace from Psalm 145

We give thanks for this good green earth and all that lives upon it.
Thanks for the air, the breath that flows from leaf to lung and back, sustaining life.
Thanks for fire, warmth in the cold season.
Thanks for water, the life-renewing rain, womb of the first life.
Thanks for soil that nourishes the grain, the wildflower and the redwood.
Thanks for the sun, life-sustaining radiance.
Thanks for the moon, for the light that drives the tides.
Thanks for our living bodies with their ability to create new life.
Thanks for the food we eat: thanks to all the beings whose death sustains our lives. Thanks to all who tend and grow our food, who plant and harvest, who bring it to us, who cook it for us with love.
Thanks for the creative spirit that continues to invent and to increase the beauty around us.
Thanks for the love and the community we share, all the acts of kindness and compassion that weave us together.
Thanks to the courage of all who stand up for the earth and for justice.
Thanks to all who say, "Yes, we will renew the land and feed the hungry; we will repair the damage and heal the wounds; we will live with open hands and open hearts, in balance and in peace."
We give thanks.
~Pagan Thanksgiving Prayer by Starhawk

O God, Source and Giver of all things,
Who does manifest Thy infinite majesty, power and goodness in all the earth, we give You honor and glory.
For the sun and the rain, for the manifold fruits of our fields,
for the increase of our herds and flocks, we thank You.
For the enrichment of our souls with divine grace, we are grateful.
Lord of the harvest, graciously accept us and the fruits of our toil, in union with Christ, Your Son,
as atonement for our sins, for the growth of Your Church,
for peace and charity in our homes. Amen.
~Catholic Harvest Prayer

Greetings to the Natural World!

Today we have gathered and we see that the cycles of life continue. We have been given the duty to live in balance and harmony with each other and all living things. So now, we bring our minds together as one as we give greetings and thanks to each other as People.
Now our minds are one. (Response of the people, like "amen.")

We are all thankful to our Mother, the Earth, for she gives us all that we need for life. She supports our feet as we walk about upon her. It gives us joy that she continues to care for us as she has from the beginning of time. To our Mother, we send greetings and thanks.
Now our minds are one.

We give thanks to all the Waters of the world for quenching our thirst and providing us with strength. Water is life. We know its power in many forms – waterfalls and rain, mists and streams, rivers and oceans. With one mind, we send greetings and thanks to the spirit of water.
Now our minds are one.

We turn our minds to all the Fish life in the water. They were instructed to cleanse and purify the water. They also give themselves to us as food. We are grateful that we can still find pure water. So we turn now to the Fish and send our greetings and thanks.
Now our minds are one.

Now we turn toward the vast fields of Plant life. As far as the eye can see, the Plants grow, working many wonders. They sustain many life forms. With our minds working together, we give thanks and look forward to seeing Plant life for many generations to come.
Now our minds are one.

With one mind, we turn to honor and thank all the Food Plants we harvest from the garden. Since the beginning of time, the grains, vegetables, beans, and berries have helped the People survive. Many other living things draw strength from them too. We gather all the Plant Foods together as one and send them a greeting and thanks.
Now our minds are one.

Now we turn to all the Medicine Herbs of the world. From the beginning, they were instructed to take away sickness. They are always waiting and ready to heal us. We are happy there are still among us those special few who remember how to use these plants for healing. With one mind, we send greetings and thanks to the Medicines and to the Keepers of the Medicines.
Now our minds are one.

We gather our minds together to send greetings and thanks to all the Animal life in the world. They have many things to teach us as People. We see them near our homes and in the deep forests. We are glad they are still here and we hope that it will always be so.
Now our minds are one.

We now turn our thoughts to the Trees. The Earth has many families of Trees who have their own instructions and uses. Some provide us with shelter and shade, others with fruit, beauty and other useful things. Many peoples of the world use a Tree as a symbol of peace and strength. With one mind, we greet and thank the Tree life.
Now our minds are one.

We put our minds together as one and thank all the Birds who move and fly about over our heads. The Creator gave them beautiful songs. Each day they remind us to enjoy and appreciate life. The Eagle was chosen to be their leader. To all the Birds, from the smallest to the largest, we send our joyful greetings and thanks.
Now our minds are one.

We are all thankful to the powers we know as the Four Winds. We hear their voices in the moving air as they refresh us and purify the air we breathe. They help to bring the change of seasons. From the four directions they come, bringing us messages and giving us strength. With one mind, we send our greetings and thanks to the Four Winds.
Now our minds are one.

Now we turn to the west where our Grandfathers, the Thunder Beings, live. With lightning and thundering voices, they bring with them the water that renews life. We bring our minds together as one to send greetings and thanks to our Grandfathers, the Thunderers.
Now our minds are one.

He is a wise man who does not grieve for the things which he has not, but rejoices for those which he has. ~Epictetus

THANKSGIVING JOY

We now send greetings and thanks to our eldest Brother, the Sun. Each day without fail he travels the sky from east to west, bringing the light of a new day. He is the source of all the fires of life. With one mind, we send greetings and thanks to our Brother, the Sun.
Now our minds are one.

We put our minds together and give thanks to our oldest Grandmother, the Moon, who lights the night-time sky. She is the leader of women all over the world, and she governs the movement of the ocean tides. By her changing face we measure time, and it is the Moon who watches over the arrival of children here on Earth. With one mind, we send greetings and thanks to our Grandmother, the Moon.
Now our minds are one.

We give thanks to the Stars who are spread across the sky like jewelry. We see them in the night, helping the Moon to light the darkness and bringing dew to the gardens and growing things. When we travel at night, they guide us home. With our minds gathered together as one, we send greetings and thanks to all the Stars.
Now our minds are one.

We gather our minds to greet and thank the enlightened Teachers who have come to help throughout the ages. When we forget how to live in harmony, they remind us of the way we were instructed to live as People. With one mind, we send greeting and thanks to these caring Teachers.
Now our minds are one.

Now we turn our thoughts to the Great Spirit, the Creator, and send greetings and thanks for the gifts of Creation. Everything we need to live a good life is here on this Mother Earth. For all the love that is still around us, we gather our minds together as one and send our finest words of greetings and thanks to the Creator.
Now our minds are one.

We have now arrived at the place where we end our words. Of all the things we have named, it was not our intention to leave anything out. If something was forgotten, we leave it to each individual to send such greetings and thanks in their own way.
Now our minds are one.
~Haudenosaunee (Iroquois) prayer

TOASTS

Here are a few quotes that would be appropriate for toasts, as well as a few tips for creating your own toast. Remember to end with "Cheers," "Salute," or another similar word so everybody knows when it's time to lift the glass to one another and drink.

May our gratitude lead to action: may we express our gratitude. May we smile when we encounter each other on the path, may we seek opportunities to share our talents with others, may we express our love to one another, may we give with no expectation of receiving. May we seek to repair what is broken. May we end each day counting the day's blessing, those we have received and those we have bestowed. May we be a blessing. (Rabbi Maralee Gordon)

Let us remember that, as much has been given us, much will be expected from us, and that true homage comes from the heart as well as from the lips, and shows itself in deeds. (Theodore Roosevelt)

But see, in our open clearings, how golden the melons lie; enrich them with sweets and spices, and give us the pumpkin pie. (Margaret Junkin Preston)

Gratitude can transform common days into thanksgivings, turn routine jobs into joy, and change ordinary opportunities into blessings. (William Arthur Ward)

Stand up, on this Thanksgiving Day, stand upon your feet. Believe in man. Soberly and with clear eyes, believe in your own time and place. There is not, and there never has been, a better time, or a better place, to live in. (Phillips Brooks)

THANKSGIVING JOY

I do not think of all the misery, but of the glory that remains. Go outside into the fields, nature and the sun, go out and seek happiness in yourself and in God. Think of the beauty that again and again discharges itself within and without you and be happy. (Anne Frank)

Gratitude unlocks the fullness of life. It turns what we have into enough, and more. It turns denial in to acceptance, chaos to order, confusion to clarity. It can turn a meal into a feast, a house into a home, a stranger into a friend. Gratitude makes sense of our past, brings peace for today and creates a vision for tomorrow. (Melody Beattie)

Dear Lord; we beg but one boon more: Peace in the hearts of all men living, peace in the whole world this Thanksgiving. (Joseph Auslander)

Got no check books, got no banks; still I'd like to express my thanks – I've got the sun in the morning and the moon at night. (Irving Berlin)

Now is no time to think of what you do not have. Think of what you can do with what there is. (Ernest Hemmingway)

The American eagle and the Thanksgiving turkey: may one give us peace in all our states, and the other, a piece for all our plates. (Unknown)

We should certainly count our blessings, but we should also make our blessings count. (Neal A. Maxwell)

Appreciation can change a day, even change a life. Your willingness to put it into words is all that is necessary. (Margaret Cousins)

Celebrate the happiness that friends are always giving, make every day a holiday and celebrate just living! (Amanda Bradley)

To America, the first community in which men set out to institutionalize freedom, responsible government, and human equality. (Adlai Stevenson)

Here's to the blessing of the year; here's to the friends we hold so dear; to peace on earth, both far and near. (Unknown)

Small cheer and great welcome makes a merry feast. (William Shakespeare)

May your stuffing be tasty, may your turkey plump, may your potatoes and gravy have nary a lump. May your yams be delicious, and your pies take the prize, and may your Thanksgiving dinner stay off your thighs! (Unknown)

Give thanks for unknown blessings already on their way. ~Native American saying

94

CREATING YOUR OWN TOAST

It can be fun to create your own toast. Many begin with a short quote, then add something they are personally thankful for. Since a toast is meant to be said in honor of someone, it is common in small gatherings to mention each person present. Conclude with an encouraging wish or hope. For example:

William Arthur Ward said, "Feeling gratitude and not expressing it is like wrapping a present and not giving it." I'd like to express my gratitude for each of you sharing this special day. David, thank you for your unfailing love and support. April, your strength encourages us all to keep on going, no matter the obstacles. Faith, your compassion is an inspiration and a vision of what a world of peace would look like. Josh, I'm so glad you're part of our family; you make it complete. Kaegan, your inquisitive mind reminds us that there is always more to learn and do. May you all continue to make the world a better place for many years to come.

Instead of mentioning personal attributes, you may wish to focus on accomplishments reached that year (or that soon will be) by those present. Here's an example:

It is wonderful to be here with you all today. As we look back over the year, we have so much to be thankful for. David, you have created a beautiful home where we all feel welcome; thank you. April and Josh, your hard work has made a success of your new business; you motivate us all to put our hearts into our work. Faith, we're so proud of your certification in yoga instruction; your tendency to help others has taken another step forward. Clint, I don't know you very well, but I'm glad you're here and appreciate what you bring to our family. Kaegan, now that you're driving, you're even busier in new adventures; you show us how life is meant to be lived. Here's to all you've accomplished, and to all you will do in the future.

In larger gatherings, it may not be appropriate to mention each person. In that case, the group as a whole may be referred to, as in the following example.

I'm thankful to be here with you all. It's remarkable that we've all made it here, together, despite our busy lives. But that's what Thanksgiving is about – friends and family, and blessings. As we enjoy the bountiful feast before us, let's remember all we have to be thankful for, and how fortunate we all are to be together on this special day. Here's to many more Thanksgivings together.

If the year was a difficult one, you can focus on the fact that you've all come through it.

I'm so happy all of you are able to be here this Thanksgiving. We've each faced some hardships this year, but here we are, still moving forward, getting stronger with each challenge. I'm thankful for the support I've received from each of you, and I want you all to know that I'm here for you. Even though some things have been rough, we still have much to be thankful for, and each of you are at the top of my list. Here's to the future and the blessings it will bring.

GIVING THANKS

PROCLAMATIONS AND HISTORIC WRITINGS

William Bradford, the second Governor of Plymouth Plantation,
wrote of the Puritans' experiences in *Of Plimoth Plantation*:

They began now to gather in ye small harvest they had, and to fit up their
houses and dwellings against winter, being all well recovered in health &
strength, and had all things in good plenty; For as some were thus employed in
affairs abroad, others were exercised in fishing, about cod, & bass, & other fish,
of which they took good store, of which every family had their portion. All
the summer there was no want. And now began to come in store of fowl, as
winter approached, of which this place did abound when they came first (but
afterward decreased by degrees). And besides water fowl, there was great store
of wild turkeys, of which they took many, besides venison, &c. Besides, they
had about a peck of meal a week to a person, or now since harvest, Indian corn
to proportion. Which made many afterwards write so largely of their plenty
here to their friends in England, which were not fained, but true reports.

Edward Winslow of Plymouth Plantation wrote the following
excerpt in December, 1621. It was published in a booklet called
Mourt's Relation:

We set the last spring some twenty acres of Indian corn, and sowed some
six acres of barley and peas, and according to the manner of the Indians, we
manured our ground with herrings or rather shads, which we have in great
abundance, and take with great ease at our doors. Our corn did prove well,
and God be praised, we had a good increase of Indian corn, and our barley
indifferent good, but our peas not worth the gathering, for we feared they were
too late sown, they came up very well, and blossomed, but the sun parched
them in the blossom; our harvest being gotten in, our governor sent four men
on fowling, that so we might after a more special manner rejoice together,
after we had gathered the fruit of our labors; they four in one day killed as
much fowl, as with a little help beside, served the company almost a week, at
which time amongst other recreations, we exercised our arms, many of the
Indians coming amongst us, and among the rest their greatest King Massasoit,
with some ninety men, whom for three days we entertained and feasted, and

By the HONOURABLE

William Dummer Efq;

Lieutenant GOVERNOUR and Commander in Chief of His
Majefty's Province of the *Maffachufetts-Bay* in *New-England* :

A Proclamation for a General
THANKSGIVING.

FORASMUCH as amidft the various & awful Rebukes of Heaven with which
we are righteoufly afflicted, We are ftill under the higheft and moft indifpenfible
Obligations of Gratitude for the many Inftances of the Divine Goodnefs in the
courfe of the Year paft, **More efpecially**, That it has pleafed Almighty GOD
to prolong the Life of our moft gracious Sovereign Lord the KING, Their
Royal Highneffes the Prince & Princefs of **Wales**, and Their Illuftrious Off-
fpring, and to give an happy Increafe to the Royal Family ; To defeat the wicked
and defperate Confpiracies againft His Majefty's Sacred Perfon and Rightful
Government, and to Direct the Councils of the Nation to fuch Meafures for the
Suppreffing & Punifhing the fame, as under GOD may prove the Means of their
lafting Quiet & Security ; So far to fucceed the Adminiftrations of His Majefty's Government in this Province,
To continue our invaluable Privileges, To reftore Health to us, To give us great Plenty of the Fruits of the
Earth, To Defeat fome Meafure the repeated Attempts of the **Indian Enemy** againft us, and to
defend fo many of our Frontier Plantations from their Rage & Fury, To guard our Sea-Coafts againft the
rapacious & bloody **Pirates**, and deliver many of them into the Hands of Juftice ; And above all that
He continues to us the precious Benefits & Liberties of the Gofpel :

I have therefore thought fit, by and with the Advice of His Majefty's Council, to
Order & Appoint that Thurfday the Twenty-eighth of November Currant be folemnly
Obferved as a Day of Publick THANKSGIVING throughout this Province,
Exhorting both Minifters and People in their refpective Affemblies to offer up
their unfeign'd THANKS to Almighty GOD for thefe and all other His un-
merited Favours. And all Servile Labour is forbidden on the faid Day.

Given at the Council Chamber in *Bofton* the Sixth Day of *November*, 1723. In the Tenth Year of the Reign
of Our Sovereign Lord GEORGE, by the Grace of GOD of *Great Britain*, *France* and *Ireland*,
KING, Defender of the Faith, &c.

By Order of the Honourable the LieutenantGovernour,
by and with the Advice of the Council,

Jofiah Willard, Secr.

W. DUMMER.

GOD Save the King.

BOSTON : Printed by B. Green,   Lieut. GOVERNOUR and COUNCIL. 1723.

they went out and killed five deer, which they brought to the plantation and bestowed on our governor, and upon the captain, and others. And although it be not always so plentiful, as it was at this time with us, yet by the goodness of God, we are so far from want, that we often wish you partakers of our plenty...

For fish and fowl, we have great abundance, our bay is full of lobsters all the summer, and affordeth variety of other fish; in September we can take a hogshead of eels in a night, with small labor, and can dig them out of their beds, all the winter we have mussels and othus [clams] at our doors: oysters we have none near, but we can have them brought by the Indians when we will; all the springtime the earth sendeth forth naturally very good sallet herbs: here are grapes, white and red, and very sweet and strong also. Strawberries, gooseberries, raspas, etc. Plums of three sorts, with black and red, being almost as good as a damson...

Governor John Carver and Massasoit agreed to a peace treaty on April 1, 1621. The terms were as follows:

1. That he (Massasoit, leader of the Wampanoag) nor any of his should do hurt to any of their (the settlers) people.

2. That if any of his did hurt any of theirs, he should send the offender, that they might punish him.

3. That if anything were taken away from any of theirs, he should cause it to be restored; and they should do the like to his.

4. If any did unjustly war against him, they would aid him; if any did war against them, he should aid them.

5. He should send to his neighbors confederates to certify them of this, that they might not wrong them, but might be likewise compromised in the conditions of peace.

6. That when their men came to them, they should leave their bows and arrows behind them.

7. That King James would esteem Massasoit (Ousamequin) as his friend and ally.

A second treaty, known as the Treaty of Mutual Protection, was agreed to on September 13, 1621. It stated:

Known all men by these present, that we whose names are underwritten, do acknowledge ourselves to be the royal subjects of king James, king of Great Britain, France, and Ireland, defender of the faith, &c. In witness whereof, and a testimonial of the same, we have subscribed our names, or marks, as follows:-

Ohquamehud	Nattawahunt	Quadaquina
Cawnacome	Caunbatant	Huttmoiden
Obbatinnua	Chikkatabak	Apannow

The first official Thanksgiving Proclamation in America was made on June 20, 1676 by the town council of Charlestown, Massachusetts. It read as follows:

The Holy God having by a long and Continual Series of his Afflictive dispensations in and by the present Warr with the Heathen Natives of this land, written and brought to pass bitter things against his own Covenant people in this wilderness, yet so that we evidently discern that in the midst of his judgements he hath remembered mercy, having remembered his Footstool in the day of his sore displeasure against us for our sins, with many singular Intimations of his Fatherly Compassion, and regard; reserving many of our Towns from Desolation Threatened, and attempted by the Enemy, and giving us especially of late with many of our Confederates many signal Advantages against them, without such Disadvantage to ourselves as formerly we have been sensible of, if it be the Lord's mercy that we are not consumed, It certainly bespeaks our positive Thankfulness, when our Enemies are in any measure disappointed or destroyed; and fearing the Lord should take notice under so many Intimations of his returning mercy, we should be found an Insensible people, as not standing before Him with Thanksgiving, as well as lading him with our Complaints in the time of pressing Afflictions:

The Council has thought meet to appoint and set apart the 29th day of this instant June, as a day of Solemn Thanksgiving and praise to God for such his Goodness and Favour, many Particulars of which mercy might be Instanced, but we doubt not those who are sensible of God's Afflictions, have been as diligent to espy him returning to us; and that the Lord may behold us as a

For love present, ills past, and good to come, may our hearts rejoice this Thanksgiving Day.
~Unknown

People offering Praise and thereby glorifying Him; the Council doth commend it to the Respective Ministers, Elders and people of this Jurisdiction; Solemnly and seriously to keep the same Beseeching that being perswaded by the mercies of God we may all, even this whole people offer up our bodies and souls as a living and acceptable Service unto God by Jesus Christ.

Below is the first national Thanksgiving Proclamation, which was made on November 1, 1777 by the Continental Congress. It named the day of Thanksgiving to be December 18 ,1777:

FORASMUCH as it is the indispensable Duty of all Men to adore the superintending Providence of Almighty God; to acknowledge with Gratitude their Obligation to him for Benefits received, and to implore such farther Blessings as they stand in Need of: And it having pleased him in his abundant Mercy, not only to continue to us the innumerable Bounties of his common Providence; but also to smile upon us in the Prosecution of a just and necessary War, for the Defense and Establishment of our unalienable Rights and Liberties; particularly in that he hath been pleased, in so great a Measure, to prosper the Means used for the Support of our Troops, and to crown our Arms with most signal success:

It is therefore recommended to the legislative or executive Powers of these UNITED STATES to set apart THURSDAY, the eighteenth Day of December next, for SOLEMN THANKSGIVING and PRAISE: That at one Time and with one Voice, the good People may express the grateful Feelings of their Hearts, and consecrate themselves to the Service of their Divine Benefactor; and that, together with their sincere Acknowledgments and Offerings, they may join the penitent Confession of their manifold Sins, whereby they had forfeited every Favor; and their humble and earnest Supplication that it may please GOD through the Merits of JESUS CHRIST, mercifully to forgive and blot them out of Remembrance; That it may please him graciously to afford his Blessing on the Governments of these States respectively, and prosper the public Council of the whole: To inspire our Commanders, both by Land and Sea, and all under them, with that Wisdom and Fortitude which may render them fit Instruments, under the Providence of Almighty GOD, to secure for these United States, the greatest of all human Blessings, INDEPENDENCE and PEACE: That it may please him, to prosper the Trade and Manufactures of the People, and the Labor of the Husbandman, that our Land may yield its Increase: To take Schools and Seminaries of Education, so necessary for cultivating the Principles of true Liberty, Virtue and Piety, under his nurturing Hand; and to prosper the Means of Religion, for the promotion and enlargement of that Kingdom, which consisteth "in Righteousness, Peace and Joy in the Holy Ghost." And it is further recommended, That servile Labor, and such Recreation, as, though at other Times innocent, may be unbecoming the Purpose of this Appointment, be omitted on so solemn an Occasion.

On October 3, 1789, President George Washington made the first Presidential Thanksgiving Proclamation:

Whereas it is the duty of all Nations to acknowledge the providence of Almighty God, to obey his will, to be grateful for his benefits, and humbly to implore his protection and favor, and Whereas both Houses of Congress have by their joint Committee requested me "to recommend to the People of the United States a day of public thanksgiving and prayer to be observed by acknowledging with grateful hearts the many signal favors of Almighty God, especially by affording them an opportunity peaceably to establish a form of government for their safety and happiness.

Now therefore I do recommend and assign Thursday the 26th day of November next to be devoted by the People of these States to the service of that great and glorious Being, who is the beneficent Author of all the good that was, that is, or that will be. That we may then all unite in rendering unto him our sincere and humble thanks, for his kind care and protection of the People of this country previous to their becoming a Nation, for the signal and manifold mercies, and the favorable interpositions of his providence, which we experienced in the course and conclusion of the late war, for the great degree of tranquility, union, and plenty, which we have since enjoyed, for the peaceable and rational manner in which we have been enabled to establish constitutions of government for our safety and happiness, and particularly the national one now lately instituted, for the civil and religious liberty with which we are blessed, and the means we have of acquiring and diffusing useful knowledge, and in general for all the great and various favors which he hath been pleased to confer upon us.

GIVING THANKS

President Abraham Lincoln made several Thanksgiving Proclamations. The first was on April 10, 1862:

A Proclamation By the President of the United States of America

It has pleased Almighty God to vouchsafe signal victories to the land and naval forces engaged in suppressing an internal rebellion, and at the same time to avert from our country the dangers of foreign intervention and invasion.

It is therefore recommended to the people of the United States that at their next weekly assemblages in their accustomed places of public worship which shall occur after notice of this proclamation shall have been received they especially acknowledge and render thanks to our Heavenly Father for these inestimable blessings, that they then and there implore spiritual consolation in behalf of all who have been brought into affliction by the casualties and calamities of sedition and civil war, and that they reverently invoke the divine guidance for our national counsels, to the end that they may speedily result in the restoration of peace, harmony, and unity throughout our borders and hasten the establishment of fraternal relations among all the countries of the earth.

Jefferson Davis, President of the Confederate States, also declared a Thanksgiving Day in 1862:

To the People of the Confederate States:

Once more upon the plains of Manassas have our armies been blessed by the Lord of Hosts with a triumph over our enemies. It is my privilege to invite you once more to His footstool, not now in the garb of fasting and sorrow, but with joy and gladness, to render thanks for the great mercies received at His hand. A few months since, and our enemies poured forth their invading legions upon our soil. They laid waste our fields, polluted our altars and violated the sanctity of our homes. Around our capital they gathered their forces, and with boastful threats, claimed it as already their prize. The brave troops which rallied to its defense have extinguished these vain hopes, and, under the guidance of the same almighty hand, have scattered our enemies and driven them back in dismay. Uniting these defeated forces and the various armies which had been ravaging our coasts with the army of invasion in Northern Virginia, our enemies have renewed their attempt to subjugate us at the very place where their first effort was defeated, and the vengeance of retributive justice has overtaken the entire host in a second and complete overthrow.

To this signal success accorded to our arms in the East has been graciously added another equally brilliant in the West. On the very day on which our forces were led to victory on the Plains of Manassas, in Virginia, the same Almighty arm assisted us to overcome our enemies at Richmond, in Kentucky. Thus, at one and the same time, have two great hostile armies been stricken down, and the wicked designs of their armies been set at naught.

In such circumstances, it is meet and right that, as a people, we should bow down in adoring thankfulness to that gracious God who has been our bulwark and defense, and to offer unto him the tribute of thanksgiving and praise. In his hand is the issue of all events, and to him should we, in an especial manner, ascribe the honor of this great deliverance.

Now, therefore, I, Jefferson Davis, President of the Confederate States, do issue this, my proclamation, setting apart Thursday, the 18th day of September inst., as a day of prayer and thanksgiving to Almighty God for the great mercies vouchsafed to our people, and more especially for the triumph of our arms at Richmond and Manassas; and I do hereby invite the people of the Confederate States to meet on that day at their respective places of public worship, and to unite in rendering thanks and praise to God for these great mercies, and to implore Him to conduct our country safely through the perils which surround us, to the final attainment of the blessings of peace and security.

Abraham Lincoln made two Proclamations of Thanksgiving in 1863. The first was made on July 15:

By the President of the United States of America, A Proclamation

It has pleased Almighty God to hearken to the supplications and prayers of an afflicted people and to vouchsafe to the Army and the Navy of the United States victories on land and on the sea so signal and so effective as to furnish reasonable grounds for augmented confidence that the Union of these States will be maintained, their Constitution preserved, and their peace and prosperity permanently restored. But these victories have been accorded not without sacrifices of life, limb, health, and liberty, incurred by brave, loyal, and patriotic citizens. Domestic affliction in every part of the country follows in the train of these fearful bereavements. It is meet and right to recognize and confess the presence of the Almighty Father and the power of His hand equally in these triumphs and in these sorrows:

Now, therefore, be it known that I do set apart Thursday, the 6th day of August next, to be observed as a day for national thanksgiving, praise, and prayer, and I invite the people of the United States to assemble on that occasion in their customary places of worship and in the forms approved by their own consciences render the homage due to the Divine Majesty for the wonderful things He has done in the nation's behalf and invoke the influence of His Holy Spirit to subdue the anger which has produced and so long sustained a needless and cruel rebellion, to change the hearts of the insurgents, to guide the counsels of the Government with wisdom adequate to so great a national emergency, and to visit with tender care and consolation throughout the length and breadth of our land all those who, through the vicissitudes of marches, voyages, battles, and sieges, have been brought to suffer in mind, body, or estate, and finally to lead the whole nation through the paths of repentance and submission to the divine will back to the perfect enjoyment of union and fraternal peace.

GIVING THANKS

Another proclamation was made by Lincoln on October 3, 1863.
This is the one that started the nation's annual tradition:

The year that is drawing towards its close, has been filled with the blessings of fruitful fields and healthful skies. To these bounties, which are so constantly enjoyed that we are prone to forget the source from which they come, others have been added, which are of so extraordinary a nature, that they cannot fail to penetrate and soften even the heart which is habitually insensible to the ever watchful providence of Almighty God.

In the midst of a civil war of unequalled magnitude and severity, which has sometimes seemed to foreign States to invite and to provoke their aggression, peace has been preserved with all nations, order has been maintained, the laws have been respected and obeyed, and harmony has prevailed everywhere except in the theatre of military conflict; while that theatre has been greatly contracted by the advancing armies and navies of the Union. Needful diversions of wealth and of strength from the fields of peaceful industry to the national defence, have not arrested the plough, the shuttle, or the ship; the axe had enlarged the borders of our settlements, and the mines, as well of iron and coal as of the precious metals, have yielded even more abundantly than heretofore. Population has steadily increased, notwithstanding the waste that has been made in the camp, the siege and the battle-field; and the country, rejoicing in the consciousness of augmented strength and vigor, is permitted to expect continuance of years with large increase of freedom.

No human counsel hath devised nor hath any mortal hand worked out these great things. They are the gracious gifts of the Most High God, who, while dealing with us in anger for our sins, hath nevertheless remembered mercy.

It has seemed to me fit and proper that they should be solemnly, reverently and gratefully acknowledged as with one heart and voice by the whole American People.

I do therefore invite my fellow citizens in every part of the United States, and also those who are at sea and those who are sojourning in foreign lands, to set apart and observe the last Thursday of November next, as a day of Thanksgiving and Praise to our beneficent Father who dwelleth in the Heavens.

And I recommend to them that while offering up the ascriptions justly due to

Him for such singular deliverances and blessings, they do also, with humble penitence for our national perverseness and disobedience, commend to his tender care all those who have become widows, orphans, mourners or sufferers in the lamentable civil strife in which we are unavoidably engaged, and fervently implore the interposition of the Almighty Hand to heal the wounds of the nation and to restore it as soon as may be consistent with the Divine purposes to the full enjoyment of peace, harmony, tranquility and Union.

President Lincoln's final Proclamation of Thanksgiving was given on October 20, 1864:

It has pleased Almighty God to prolong our national life another year, defending us with his guardian care against unfriendly designs from abroad, and vouchsafing to us in His mercy many and signal victories over the enemy, who is of our own household. It has also pleased our Heavenly Father to favor as well our citizens in their homes as our soldiers in their camps and our sailors on the rivers and seas with unusual health. He has largely augmented our free population by emancipation and by immigration, while he has opened to us new sources of wealth, and has crowned the labor of our working men in every department of industry with abundant rewards. Moreover, He has been pleased to animate and inspire our minds and hearts with fortitude, courage and resolution sufficient for the great trial of civil war into which we have been brought by our adherence as a nation to the cause of Freedom and Humanity, and to afford to us reasonable hopes of an ultimate and happy deliverance from all our dangers and afflictions.

Now, therefore, I, Abraham Lincoln, President of the United States, do, hereby, appoint and set apart the last Thursday in November next as a day, which I desire to be observed by all my fellow-citizens wherever they may then be as a day of Thanksgiving and Praise to Almighty God the beneficent Creator and Ruler of the Universe. And I do farther recommend to my fellow-citizens aforesaid that on that occasion they do reverently humble themselves in the dust and from thence offer up penitent and fervent prayers and supplications to the Great Disposer of events for a return of the inestimable blessings of Peace, Union and Harmony throughout the land, which it has pleased Him to assign as a dwelling place for ourselves and for our posterity throughout all generations.

GIVING THANKS

The Great Binding Law, from the Constitution of the Iroquois Nations:

Whenever the Confederate Lords shall assemble for the purpose of holding a council, the Onondaga Lords shall open it by expressing their gratitude to their cousin Lords and greeting them,

then they shall make an address and offer thanks to the earth where men dwell, to the streams of water, the pools, the springs and the lakes, to the maize and the fruits, to the medicinal herbs and trees, to the forest trees for their usefulness, to the animals that serve as food and give their pelts for clothing, to the great winds and the lesser winds, to the Thunderers, to the Sun, the mighty warrior, to the moon, to the messengers of the Creator who reveal his wishes and to the Great Creator who dwells in the heavens above, who gives all the things useful to men, and who is the source and the ruler of health and life.

Then shall the Onondaga Lords declare the council open.

POEMS

THANKSGIVING TIME

When the night winds whistle through the trees and blow the crisp brown
leaves a-crackling down,
When the autumn moon is big and yellow-orange and round,
When old Jack Frost is sparkling on the ground,
    It's Thanksgiving Time!

When the pantry jars are full of mince-meat and the shelves are laden with
sweet spices for a cake,
When the butcher man sends up a turkey nice and fat to bake,
When the stores are crammed with everything ingenious cooks can make,
    It's Thanksgiving Time!

When the gales of coming winter outside your window howl,
When the air is sharp and cheery so it drives away your scowl,
When one's appetite craves turkey and will have no other fowl,
    It's Thanksgiving Time!

~Langston Hughes

HOW TO OBSERVE THANKSGIVING

Count your blessings instead of your crosses;
Count your gains instead of your losses.

Count your joys instead of your woes;
Count your friends instead of your foes.

Count your smiles instead of your tears;
Count your courage instead of your fears.

Count your full years instead of your lean;
Count your kind deeds instead of your mean.

Count your health instead of your wealth;
Count on God instead of yourself.

~Unknown

GIVING THANKS

FATHER WE THANK THEE

For flowers that bloom about our feet,
Father, we thank Thee.
For tender grass so fresh, so sweet,
Father, we thank Thee.
For the song of bird and hum of bee,
For all things fair we hear or see,
Father in heaven, we thank Thee.

For blue of stream and blue of sky,
Father, we thank Thee.
For pleasant shade of branches high,
Father, we thank Thee.
For fragrant air and cooling breeze,
For beauty of the blooming trees,
Father in heaven, we thank Thee.

For this new morning with its light,
Father, we thank Thee.
For rest and shelter of the night,
Father, we thank Thee
For health and food, for love and friends,
For everything Thy goodness sends,
Father in heaven, we thank Thee.

~ Unknown, often misattributed to Ralph Waldo Emerson

For wealth and plenty in the land
For faith in God's sustaining hand
For every blessing great and small
We thank the Giver of it all.

~Unknown

For nuts and pears and apples, and everything we need,
For pumpkin pie and turkey, we give Thee thanks indeed.
~Unknown

THANKSGIVING

Gettin' together to smile an' rejoice,
An' eatin' an' laughin' with folks of your choice;
An' kissin' the girls an' declarin' that they
Are growin' more beautiful day after day;
Chattin' an' braggin' a bit with the men,
Buildin' the old family circle again;
Livin' the wholesome an' old-fashioned cheer,
Just for a while at the end of the year.

Greetings fly fast as we crowd through the door
And under the old roof we gather once more
Just as we did when the youngsters were small;
Mother's a little bit grayer, that's all.
Father's a little bit older, but still
Ready to romp an' to laugh with a will.
Here we are back at the table again
Tellin' our stories as women an' men.

Bowed are our heads for a moment in prayer;
Oh, but we're grateful an' glad to be there.
Home from the east land an' home from the west,
Home with the folks that are dearest an' best.
Out of the sham of the cities afar
We've come for a time to be just what we are.
Here we can talk of ourselves an' be frank,
Forgettin' position an' station an' rank.

Give me the end of the year an' its fun
When most of the plannin' an' toilin' is done;
Bring all the wanderers home to the nest,
Let me sit down with the ones I love best,
Hear the old voices still ringin' with song,
See the old faces unblemished by wrong,
See the old table with all of its chairs
An' I'll put soul in my Thanksgivin' prayers.

~Edgar Albert Guest

Reflect on your present blessings, of which every man has many; not on your past misfortunes, of which all men have some. ~Charles Dickens

GIVING THANKS

AN AUTUMN EVENING

Dark hills against a hollow crocus sky
Scarfed with its crimson pennons, and below
The dome of sunset long, hushed valleys lie
Cradling the twilight, where the lone winds blow
And wake among the harps of leafless trees
Fantastic runes and mournful melodies.

The chilly purple air is threaded through
With silver from the rising moon afar,
And from a gulf of clear, unfathomed blue
In the southwest glimmers a great gold star
Above the darkening druid glens of fir
Where beckoning boughs and elfin voices stir.

And so I wander through the shadows still,
And look and listen with a rapt delight,
Pausing again and yet again at will
To drink the elusive beauty of the night,
Until my soul is filled, as some deep cup,
That with divine enchantment is brimmed up.

~Lucy Maud Montgomery

TO AUTUMN (I)

Season of mists and mellow fruitfulness,
  Close bosom-friend of the maturing sun;
Conspiring with him how to load and bless
  With fruit the vines that round the thatch-eaves run;
To bend with apples the moss'd cottage-trees,
  And fill all fruit with ripeness to the core;
To swell the gourd, and plump the hazel shells
  With a sweet kernel; to set budding more,
And still more, later flowers for the bees,
  Until they think warm days will never cease,
For summer has o'er-brimm'd their clammy cells.

~John Keats

FOR THE BEAUTY OF THE EARTH

For the beauty of the earth,
for the glory of the skies,
for the love which from our birth
over and around us lies;
Lord of all, to Thee we raise
this our hymn of grateful praise.

For the beauty of each hour
of the day and of the night,
hill and vale, and tree and flower,
sun and moon, and stars of light;
Lord of all, to Thee we raise
this our hymn of grateful praise.

For the joy of ear and eye,
for the heart and mind's delight,
for the mystic harmony,
linking sense to sound and sight;
Lord of all, to Thee we raise
this our hymn of grateful praise.

For the joy of human love,
brother, sister, parent, child,
friends on earth and friends above,
for all gentle thoughts and mild;
Lord of all, to Thee we raise
this our hymn of grateful praise.

For Thy church, that evermore
lifteth holy hands above,
offering upon every shore
her pure sacrifice of love;
Lord of all, to Thee we raise
this our hymn of grateful praise.

For Thyself, best Gift Divine,
to the world so freely given,

GIVING THANKS

for that great, great love of Thine,
peace on earth, and joy in heaven:
Lord of all, to Thee we raise
this our hymn of grateful praise.

~ Folliot S. Pierpoint

THANKSGIVING DAY

Come gather round the table
To say a happy grace,
For family and food and friends
And a smile on every face.

The harvest now is over,
The fields are clean and bare,
For all the fruits are gathered in
And stored away with care.

Be thankful for the harvest,
For friends so good and gay,
For happiness and loving care
On this Thanksgiving Day.

~Kathryn S. Gibson

THANKSGIVING JOY

THANKSGIVING

The year has turned its circle,
The seasons come and go.
The harvest all is gathered in
And chilly north winds blow.
Orchards have shared their treasures,
The fields, their yellow grain,
So open wide the doorway ---
Thanksgiving comes again!

~Unknown

THANKSGIVING TIME

When all the leaves are off the boughs,
And nuts and apples gathered in,
And cornstalks waiting for the cows,
And pumpkins safe in barn and bin,
Then Mother says, "My children dear,
The fields are brown, and autumn flies;
Thanksgiving Day is very near,
And we must make thanksgiving pies!"

~Unknown

THE PUMPKIN

Oh, greenly and fair in the lands of the sun,
The vines of the gourd and the rich melon run,
And the rock and the tree and the cottage enfold,
With broad leaves all greenness and blossoms all gold,
Like that which o'er Nineveh's prophet once grew,
While he waited to know that his warning was true,
And longed for the storm-cloud, and listened in vain
For the rush of the whirlwind and red fire-rain.

116

GIVING THANKS

On the banks of the Xenil the dark Spanish maiden
Comes up with the fruit of the tangled vine laden;
And the Creole of Cuba laughs out to behold
Through orange-leaves shining the broad spheres of gold;
Yet with dearer delight from his home in the North,
On the fields of his harvest the Yankee looks forth,
Where crook-necks are coiling and yellow fruit shines,
And the sun of September melts down on his vines.

Ah! on Thanksgiving day, when from East and from West,
From North and from South comes the pilgrim and guest;
When the gray-haired New Englander sees round his board
The old broken links of affection restored;
When the care-wearied man seeks his mother once more,
And the worn matron smiles where the girl smiled before;
What moistens the lip and what brightens the eye,
What calls back the past, like the rich Pumpkin pie?

Oh, fruit loved of boyhood! the old days recalling,
When wood-grapes were purpling and brown nuts were falling!
When wild, ugly faces we carved in its skin,
Glaring out through the dark with a candle within!
When we laughed round the corn-heap, with hearts all in tune,
Our chair a broad pumpkin, -- our lantern the moon,
Telling tales of the fairy who travelled like steam
In a pumpkin-shell coach, with two rats for her team!

Then thanks for thy present! none sweeter or better
E'er smoked from an oven or circled a platter!
Fairer hands never wrought at a pastry more fine,
Brighter eyes never watched o'er its baking, than thine!
And the prayer, which my mouth is too full to express,
Swells my heart that thy shadow may never be less,
That the days of thy lot may be lengthened below,
And the fame of thy worth like a pumpkin-vine grow,
And thy life be as sweet, and its last sunset sky
Golden-tinted and fair as thy own Pumpkin pie!

~John Greenleaf Whittier

THANKSGIVING

We walk on starry fields of white
And do not see the daisies;
For blessings common in our sight
We rarely offer praises.
We sigh for some supreme delight
To crown our lives with splendor,
And quite ignore our daily store
Of pleasures sweet and tender.

Our cares are bold and push their way
Upon our thought and feeling.
They hang about us all the day,
Our time from pleasure stealing.
So unobtrusive many a joy
We pass by and forget it,
But worry strives to own our lives
And conquers if we let it.

There's not a day in all the year
But holds some hidden pleasure,
And looking back, joys oft appear
To brim the past's wide measure.
But blessings are like friends, I hold,
Who love and labor near us.
We ought to raise our notes of praise
While living hearts can hear us.

Full many a blessing wears the guise
Of worry or of trouble.
Farseeing is the soul and wise
Who knows the mask is double.
But he who has the faith and strength
To thank his God for sorrow
Has found a joy without alloy
To gladden every morrow.

GIVING THANKS

We ought to make the moments notes
Of happy, glad Thanksgiving;
The hours and days a silent phrase
Of music we are living.
And so the theme should swell and grow
As weeks and months pass o'er us,
And rise sublime at this good time,
A grand Thanksgiving chorus.

~Ella Wheeler Wilcox

Thanks are the highest form of thought, and gratitude is happiness doubled by wonder. ~ G.K. Chesterton

119

A THANKSGIVING POEM

The sun hath shed its kindly light,
Our harvesting is gladly o'er,
Our fields have felt no killing blight,
Our bins are filled with goodly store.

From pestilence, fire, flood, and sword
We have been spared by Thy decree,
And now with humble hearts, O Lord,
We come to pay our thanks to Thee.

We feel that had our merits been
The measure of Thy gifts to us,
We erring children, born of sin,
Might not now be rejoicing thus.

No deed of ours hath brought us grace;
When Thou wert nigh our sight was dull,
We hid in trembling from Thy face,
But Thou, O God, wert merciful.

Thy mighty hand o'er all the land
Hath still been open to bestow
Those blessings which our wants demand
From heaven, whence all blessings flow.

Thou hast, with ever watchful eye,
Looked down on us with holy care,
And from Thy storehouse in the sky
Hast scattered plenty everywhere.

Then lift we up our songs of praise
To Thee, O Father, good and kind;
To Thee we consecrate our days;
Be Thine the temple of each mind.

With incense sweet our thanks ascend;
Before Thy works our powers pall;
Though we should strive years without end,
We could not thank Thee for them all.

~Paul Laurence Dunbar

120

NOVEMBER EVENING

Come, for the dusk is our own; let us fare forth together,
With a quiet delight in our hearts for the ripe, still, autumn weather,
Through the rustling valley and wood and over the crisping meadow,
Under a high-sprung sky, winnowed of mist and shadow.

Sharp is the frosty air, and through the far hill-gaps showing
Lucent sunset lakes of crocus and green are glowing;
'Tis the hour to walk at will in a wayward, unfettered roaming,
Caring for naught save the charm, elusive and swift, of the gloaming.

Watchful and stirless the fields as if not unkindly holding
Harvested joys in their clasp, and to their broad bosoms folding
Baby hopes of a Spring, trusted to motherly keeping,
Thus to be cherished and happed through the long months of their sleeping.

Silent the woods are and gray; but the firs than ever are greener,
Nipped by the frost till the tang of their loosened balsam is keener;
And one little wind in their boughs, eerily swaying and swinging,
Very soft and low, like a wandering minstrel is singing.

Beautiful is the year, but not as the springlike maiden
Garlanded with her hopes¬rather the woman laden
With wealth of joy and grief, worthily won through living,
Wearing her sorrow now like a garment of praise and thanksgiving.

Gently the dark comes down over the wild, fair places,
The whispering glens in the hills, the open, starry spaces;
Rich with the gifts of the night, sated with questing and dreaming,
We turn to the dearest of paths where the star of the homelight is gleaming.

~Lucy Maud Montgomery

STORIES

THE KING'S THANKSGIVING by Carolyn Sherwin Bailey

Every child in the village was very much excited on account of the news that had come down from the castle on the hill.

Because it had been such a rich harvest, the fields yellow with grain and the orchards crimson with fruit, the King was going to keep a thanksgiving day. He was going to ask some child from the village to come up the hill to the castle and eat dinner with the Prince and Princess. It was rumored, too, that this child would be given good gifts by the King. But it must be a very special kind of child indeed. That they all knew.

Then the village children remembered everything that had been told them by their mothers, and their grandmothers, and their great-grandmothers about the castle kitchen. Scores of cooks and scullery boys were kept busy there night and day. The fires always glowed to roast the rich fowls that turned on the spits. The cake bowls and the soup pots were never empty. Spices and herbs from far countries, strawberries when the ground was covered with snow, ices of all the rainbow colors, and cream so thick that a knife could cut it—all these were to be found in the King's kitchen.

There were dishes of gold and silver upon which to serve the fine foods, and a hothouse of rare flowers with which to deck the table, and linen as fine as a cobweb and as beautiful in pattern as snowflakes to cover it. Oh, a thanksgiving day in the castle would be very wonderful indeed, the children thought, and each hoped that he or she would be chosen to go.

The day before this day of thanksgiving the messenger of the King came down from the castle and went from door to door of the homes in the village. He went first to the house of the burgomaster. It was a very pretentious house with tall pillars in front, and it stood on a wide street. It seemed likely that the burgomaster's child might be chosen to go with the messenger to the castle for the thanksgiving. She was dressed in silk, and her hair was curled, and the burgomaster had packed a great hamper with sweets as an offering for the King.

"Are you ready to keep the feast as the King would like you to?" asked the messenger.

"Oh, yes!" said the burgomaster's child. "I have on my best dress, and here are plenty of sweets to eat. Will you take me?"

But the messenger shook his head, for the child was not ready.

Then the King's messenger went on until he came to the house where the captain of the guards lived. The captain's little boy was quite sure that he would be chosen to go with the messenger to the castle for the thanksgiving. He wore a uniform with silver braid and buttons like that which the guards wore. A sword hung at his side, and he wore a soldier's cap. He held the cap in his hand, so that he could put it on quickly.

"Are you ready to keep the thanksgiving day as the King would like you to?" asked the messenger.

"Oh, yes!" said the child of the captain of the guards. "I have my sword here and I can fight any one who crosses our path on the way to the castle. Will you take me?"

But the messenger went on again and he came to the baker's shop. The baker's boy stood at the door, dressed in his best white suit, and holding an empty basket on his arm. He was quite sure that he would be chosen to go to the palace, for his father's bake shop was an important place in the village. They measured their flour carefully, and weighed the loaves so that they might receive the utmost penny for each. They very seldom had any crumbs left for the poor, but they were selling a great deal of bread every day.

"Are you ready to keep the thanksgiving day as the King would like you to?" the messenger asked of the baker's boy.

"Oh, yes!" the boy said. "I have this basket to gather up whatever remains of the King's feast and bring it home with me. The King would not want anything wasted. Will you take me?"

But the messenger shook his head a third time, for the child was not ready.

Then he did not know which way to go, and he began to think that he would not be able to find any guest for the King's feast. As he waited, he saw two children, a girl and a boy, coming toward him. They were poor children, and one was leading the other, for he was lame. The messenger looked at them. The little girl had eyes like stars and her hair, blowing in the November wind, was like a cloud made golden by the sunset. She held her head so high, and smiled so bravely that no one would have noticed her old dress and the holes in her coat. The messenger stood in the road in front of her and spoke to her.

"Are you ready to keep the thanksgiving day as the King would like you to?" he asked.

The little girl looked up in the messenger's face in surprise.

"No, I am not ready," she said, "but this child is. I am bringing him because he is lame, and because he is hungry. Will you take him?" she asked.

"Yes," said the messenger, "and you, too. There is room at the King's table for both."

Let us offer the sacrifice of praise to God continually, that is, the fruit of our lips giving thanks to His name. ~Hebrews 13:15

GIVING THANKS

THE GIFTS OF THE LITTLE PEOPLE, An Iroquois Legend

There once was a boy whose parents had died. He lived with his uncle who did not treat him well. The uncle dressed the boy in rags, and because of this the boy was called Dirty Clothes.

This boy, Dirty Clothes, was a good hunter. He would spend many hours in the forest hunting food for his lazy uncle, who would not hunt for himself.

One day Dirty Clothes walked near the river, two squirrels that he had shot hanging from his belt. He walked near the cliffs which rose from the water. This is where the Little People, the Jo-Ge-Oh, often beat their drums. Most of the hunters from the village were afraid to go near this place, but Dirty Clothes remembered the words his mother had spoken years ago, "Whenever you walk with good in your heart, you should never be afraid."

A hickory tree grew there near the river. He saw something moving in its branches. A black squirrel as hopping about high up in the top of the tree. Then Dirty Clothes heard a small voice. "Shoot again, Brother," the small voice said. "You still have not hit him."

Dirty Clothes looked down and there near his feet were two small hunters. As he watched, one of them shot an arrow; but it fell short of the black squirrel. "Ah," Dirty Clothes thought, "they will never succeed like that. I must help them." He drew his bow and with one shot brought down the squirrel.

The tiny hunters ran to the squirrel. "Whose arrow is this?" asked one of them. They looked up and saw the boy. "Eee-yah," said one of the tiny hunters, "you have shot well. The squirrel is yours."

"Thank you," Dirty Clothes answered, "but the squirrel is yours and also these others I have shot today."

The two small hunters were very glad. "Come with us," they said. "Come visit our lodge so we can thank you properly."

Dirty Clothes thought about his uncle, but it was still early in the day and he could hunt some more after visiting them. "I'll come with you," he said.

The two Little People led the boy to the river. There a tiny canoe was waiting, only as big as one of his shoes, but his friends told him to step inside. He took one step... and found he had become as small as the tiny hunters and was sitting with them inside their canoe.

The Little People dipped their paddles and up the canoe rose into the air! It flew above the hickory tree, straight to the cliffs and into a cave, the place where the Jo-Ge-Oh people lived. There the two hunters told their story to the other Little People gathered there, who greeted the boy as a friend. "You must stay with us," his new friends said, "for just a short time, so we can teach you."

Then the Jo-Ge-Oh taught Dirty Clothes things he had never known. They told him many useful things about the birds and the forest animals. They taught him much about the corn and the squash and the beans which feed human life. They taught him about the strawberries which glow each June like embers in the grass and showed him how to make a special drink which the Little People love.

Last they showed him a new dance to teach his people, a dance to be done in a darkened place so the little People could come and dance with them unseen, a dance which would honor the Jo-Ge-Oh and thank them for their gifts.

Four days passed and the boy knew that the time had come for him to leave. "I must go to my village," he told his friends.

So it was that with the two small hunters he set out walking towards his home. As they walked with him, his two friends pointed to the many plants which were useful and the boy looked at each plant carefully, remembering its name. Later, when he turned to look back at his friends, he found himself standing all alone in a field near the edge of his village.

Dirty Clothes walked into his village wondering how so many things had changed in just four days. It was the same place, yet nothing was the same. People watched him as he walked and finally a woman came up to him. "You are welcome here, Stranger," said the woman. "Please tell us who you are."

"Don't you know?" he answered. 'I am Dirty Clothes."

"But your clothing is so beautiful," said the woman.

At that, he saw his old rags were gone. The thing he wore now was of fine new buckskin, embroidered with moose hair and porcupine quills. "Where is my uncle," he asked the woman, "who lived there in that lodge and had a nephew dressed in rags?"

Then an old man spoke up from the crowd. "He's been dead many years. Why would a fine warrior like you look for such a man?"

Dirty Clothes looked at himself and saw he was no longer a boy. He had become a full-grown man and towered over the people of his village. "I see," he said, "the Little People have given me more gifts than I thought." And he began to tell his story.

The wisest of the old men and women listened well to this young warrior. They learned many things by so listening. That night all his people did the Dark Dance to thank the Jo-Ge-Oh for their gifts and, in the darkness of the lodge, they heard the voices of the Little People joining in the song, glad to know that the human beings were grateful for their gifts. And so it is, even to this day, that the Little People remain the friends of the people of the longhouse. They work and play together, and the Dark Dance is done.

THE BOOK OF RUTH, from *The Holy Bible*

1-1 In the days when the judges ruled, there was a famine in the land. So a man from Bethlehem in Judah, together with his wife and two sons, went to live for a while in the country of Moab.

2 The man's name was Elimelek, his wife's name was Naomi, and the names of his two sons were Mahlon and Kilion. They were Ephrathites from Bethlehem, Judah. And they went to Moab and lived there.

3 Now Elimelek, Naomi's husband, died, and she was left with her two sons.

4 They married Moabite women, one named Orpah and the other Ruth. After they had lived there about ten years,

5 both Mahlon and Kilion also died, and Naomi was left without her two sons and her husband.

6 When Naomi heard in Moab that the Lord had come to the aid of his people by providing food for them, she and her daughters-in-law prepared to return home from there...

22 So Naomi returned from Moab accompanied by Ruth the Moabite, her daughter-in-law, arriving in Bethlehem as the barley harvest was beginning.

2-1 Now Naomi had a relative on her husband's side, a man of standing from the clan of Elimelek, whose name was Boaz.

2 And Ruth the Moabite said to Naomi, "Let me go to the fields and pick up the leftover grain behind anyone in whose eyes I find favor."

Naomi said to her, "Go ahead, my daughter."

3 So she went out, entered a field and began to glean behind the harvesters. As it turned out, she was working in a field belonging to Boaz, who was from the clan of Elimelek.

4 Just then Boaz arrived from Bethlehem and greeted the harvesters, "The LORD be with you!"

"The LORD bless you!" they answered.

5 Boaz asked the overseer of his harvesters, "Who does that young woman belong to?"

6 The overseer replied, "She is the Moabite who came back from Moab with Naomi.

7 She said, 'Please let me glean and gather among the sheaves behind the harvesters.' She came into the field and has remained here from morning till now, except for a short rest in the shelter."

8 So Boaz said to Ruth, "My daughter, listen to me. Don't go and glean in another field and don't go away from here. Stay here with the women who work for me.

9 Watch the field where the men are harvesting, and follow along after the women. I have told the men not to lay a hand on you. And whenever you are thirsty, go and get a drink from the water jars the men have filled."

10 At this, she bowed down with her face to the ground. She asked him, "Why have I found such favor in your eyes that you notice me—a foreigner?"

11 Boaz replied, "I've been told all about what you have done for your mother-in-law since the death of your husband—how you left your father and mother and your homeland and came to live with a people you did not know before.

12 May the LORD repay you for what you have done. May you be richly rewarded by the LORD, the God of Israel, under whose wings you have come to take refuge."

13 "May I continue to find favor in your eyes, my lord," she said. "You have put me at ease by speaking kindly to your servant—though I do not have the standing of one of your servants."

14 At mealtime Boaz said to her, "Come over here. Have some bread and dip it in the wine vinegar."

When she sat down with the harvesters, he offered her some roasted grain. She

ate all she wanted and had some left over.

15 As she got up to glean, Boaz gave orders to his men, "Let her gather among the sheaves and don't reprimand her.

16 Even pull out some stalks for her from the bundles and leave them for her to pick up, and don't rebuke her."

17 So Ruth gleaned in the field until evening. Then she threshed the barley she had gathered, and it amounted to about an ephah.

18 She carried it back to town, and her mother-in-law saw how much she had gathered. Ruth also brought out and gave her what she had left over after she had eaten enough.

19 Her mother-in-law asked her, "Where did you glean today? Where did you work? Blessed be the man who took notice of you!"

Then Ruth told her mother-in-law about the one at whose place she had been working. "The name of the man I worked with today is Boaz," she said.

20 "The LORD bless him!" Naomi said to her daughter-in-law. "He has not stopped showing his kindness to the living and the dead." She added, "That man is our close relative; he is one of our guardian-redeemers."

21 Then Ruth the Moabite said, "He even said to me, 'Stay with my workers until they finish harvesting all my grain.'"

22 Naomi said to Ruth her daughter-in-law, "It will be good for you, my daughter, to go with the women who work for him, because in someone else's field you might be harmed."

23 So Ruth stayed close to the women of Boaz to glean until the barley and wheat harvests were finished. And she lived with her mother-in-law.

3-1 One day Ruth's mother-in-law Naomi said to her, "My daughter, I must find a home for you, where you will be well provided for.

2 Now Boaz, with whose women you have worked, is a relative of ours. Tonight he will be winnowing barley on the threshing floor.

3 Wash, put on perfume, and get dressed in your best clothes. Then go down to the threshing floor, but don't let him know you are there until he has finished eating and drinking.

4 When he lies down, note the place where he is lying. Then go and uncover

his feet and lie down. He will tell you what to do."

5 "I will do whatever you say," Ruth answered.

6 So she went down to the threshing floor and did everything her mother-in-law told her to do.

7 When Boaz had finished eating and drinking and was in good spirits, he went over to lie down at the far end of the grain pile. Ruth approached quietly, uncovered his feet and lay down.

8 In the middle of the night something startled the man; he turned—and there was a woman lying at his feet!

9 "Who are you?" he asked.

"I am your servant Ruth," she said. "Spread the corner of your garment over me, since you are a guardian-redeemer of our family."

10 "The LORD bless you, my daughter," he replied. "This kindness is greater than that which you showed earlier: You have not run after the younger men, whether rich or poor.

11 And now, my daughter, don't be afraid. I will do for you all you ask. All the people of my town know that you are a woman of noble character...

15 He also said, "Bring me the shawl you are wearing and hold it out." When she did so, he poured into it six measures of barley and placed the bundle on her. Then he went back to town.

16 When Ruth came to her mother-in-law, Naomi asked, "How did it go, my daughter?"

Then she told her everything Boaz had done for her

17 and added, "He gave me these six measures of barley, saying, 'Don't go back to your mother-in-law empty-handed.'"

18 Then Naomi said, "Wait, my daughter, until you find out what happens. For the man will not rest until the matter is settled today."...

4-9 Then Boaz announced to the elders and all the people, "Today you are witnesses that I have bought from Naomi all the property of Elimelek, Kilion and Mahlon.

10 I have also acquired Ruth the Moabite, Mahlon's widow, as my wife, in

Be grateful for every good thing that comes to you, and give thanks continuously. And because all things have contributed to your advancement, include all things in your gratitude. ~ Ralph Waldo Emerson

order to maintain the name of the dead with his property, so that his name will not disappear from among his family or from his hometown. Today you are witnesses!"

11 Then the elders and all the people at the gate said, "We are witnesses. May the LORD make the woman who is coming into your home like Rachel and Leah, who together built up the family of Israel. May you have standing in Ephrathah and be famous in Bethlehem.

12 Through the offspring the LORD gives you by this young woman, may your family be like that of Perez, whom Tamar bore to Judah."

13 So Boaz took Ruth and she became his wife. When he made love to her, the LORD enabled her to conceive, and she gave birth to a son.

14 The women said to Naomi: "Praise be to the LORD, who this day has not left you without a guardian-redeemer. May he become famous throughout Israel!

15 He will renew your life and sustain you in your old age. For your daughter-in-law, who loves you and who is better to you than seven sons, has given him birth."

16 Then Naomi took the child in her arms and cared for him.

17 The women living there said, "Naomi has a son!" And they named him Obed. He was the father of Jesse, the father of David.

THE THANKSGIVING GOOSE by Fannie Wilder Brown

But I don't like roast goose," said Guy, pouting. "I'd rather have turkey. Turkey is best for Thanksgiving, anyway. Goose is for Christmas."

Guy's mother did not answer. He watched her while she carefully wrote G. T. W. on the corner of a pretty new red-bordered handkerchief. Five others, all alike, and all marked alike, lay beside it. The initials were his own.

"Why didn't you buy some blue ones? I'd rather have them different," he said.

Mrs. Wright smiled a queer little smile, but did not answer. She lighted a large lamp and held the marked corner of one of the handkerchiefs against the hot chimney. The heat made the indelible ink turn dark, although the writing had been so faint Guy hardly could see it before.

"Oh, dear," he cried, "there's a little blot at the top of that T! I don't want to carry a handkerchief that has a blot on it."

"Very well," said his mother. "I'll put them away, and you may carry your old ones until you ask me to let you carry this one. I don't care to furnish new things for a boy who doesn't appreciate them."

"I don't like old—"
"That will do, Guy. Never mind the rest of the things that you don't like. I want you to take this dollar down to Mrs. Burns. Tell her that I shall have a day's work for her on Friday, and I thought she might like to have part of the pay in advance to help make Thanksgiving with. Please go now."

"But a dollar won't help much. She won't like that. She always acts just as if she was as happy as anybody. I don't want to go there on such an errand as that."

Mrs. Wright smiled again, but her tone was very grave. "Mrs. Burns is 'as happy as anybody,' Guy, and she has the best-behaved children in the neighborhood. The little ones almost never cry, and I never have seen the older ones quarrel. But there are eight children, and Mr. Burns has only one arm, so he can't earn much money. Mrs. Burns has to turn her hands to all sorts of things to keep the children clothed and fed. She'll be thankful to get the dollar—you see if she isn't! And tell her if she is making mince pies to sell this year, I'll take three."

Guy walked very slowly down the street until he came to the little house where the Burns family lived.

"I'd hate to live here," he thought. "I don't see where they all sleep. My room isn't big enough, but I don't believe there's a room in this house as big as mine. I shouldn't have a bit of fun, ever, if I lived here. And I'd hate to have my mother make pies and send me about to sell them."

Then he knocked on the front door, for there was no bell. No one came. He could hear people talking in the distance, so he knew some of the family were at home. Someone always was at home here to look after the little children. He walked around to the kitchen door: it stood open. The children were talking so fast they did not hear his knock.

They were very busy. Katie, the eleven-year-old, and Malcolm, ten, Guy's age, were cutting citron into long, thin strips, piling it on a big blue plate. Mary and James, the eight-year-old twins, were paring apples with a paring machine. The long, curling skins fell in a large stone jar standing on a clean paper, spread on the floor. Charlie, who was only four years old, was watching to see that none of the parings fell over the edge of the jar. Susan, who was seven, was putting raisins, a few at a time, into a meat chopper screwed down on the kitchen table. George, three years old, was turning the handle of the chopper to grind the raisins. Baby Joe was creeping about the kitchen floor after a kitten. Mrs. Burns was taking a great piece of meat from a steaming kettle on the back of the stove. Everyone was working, except the baby and the kitten, but all seemed to be having a glorious time. What they were saying seemed so funny it was some time before Guy could understand it. At last he was sure it was some kind of a game.

"Mice?" asked Susan. Mary squealed, and they all laughed.

"Because they're small," said Mary. "Snakes?"

"They can't climb trees," Mrs. Burns called out from the pantry. The children fairly roared at that.

"A pantry with no window in it?"

"Oh, we've had that before," Katie answered. "I know what you say. It's a good place to ripen pears in when Mrs. Wright gives us some."

Guy knocked very loudly at that. He had not thought that he was listening.

The children started, but did not leave their work. They looked at their mother. "Jamie," she said. Then Jamie came to meet Guy, and invited him to walk in.

134

"What game is it?" asked Guy, forgetting his errand.

"Making mince pies," said Jamie. "It's lots of fun. Don't you want to play? I'll let you turn the paring machine if you'd like that best."

Guy said "Thank you" and began to turn the parer eagerly. "But I don't mean what you are doin'," said Guy. "I knew that was mince pies. I thought that was work. I meant what you were saying. It sounds so funny! I never heard it before."

"Mamma made it up," explained Malcolm. "It's great fun. We always play it at Thanksgiving time. You think of something that people don't like, and the one who can think first tells what he is thankful for about it. We call it 'Thanksgiving.'"

Guy stayed for an hour, and played both games. Then, quite to his surprise, the twelve o'clock whistles blew, and he had to go home. But he remembered his errands and did them, to the great pleasure of the whole Burns family.

In the afternoon Guy spent some time writing a note to his mother. It was badly written, but it made his mother happy. It read:

Dear Mother:—I am Thankful the blot isent any bigger. I am Thankful the hankershefs isent black on the borders. I would like that one with the Blot on to put in my pocket when you read this. But my old ones are nice. The Burnses dont have things to be Thankful for but they are Thankful just the same. I am Thankful for the Goose we are going to have. The best is I am Thankful I am not a Goose myself, for if I was I wouldent know enough to be Thankful.

WHY THE TURKEY GOBBLES, A Cherokee Legend

In the old times, the animals and birds liked to play ball, and they shouted and hallooed just as players do today.

The Grouse used to have a fine voice and could shout very loud at the ball-game; but the Turkey could make no noise at all.

One day the Turkey asked the Grouse to teach him how to use his voice, and the Grouse agreed to do so in return for a ruffle of feathers to wear about his neck. The Turkey gave him a fine one, and that is how the Grouse got his collar of feathers.

They began the lessons, and the Turkey learned very fast. By and by the Grouse thought it was time to try the Turkey's voice at a distance, to see how far he could shout.

"You go over by yonder tree and I'll stand on this hollow log. When I give the signal by tapping on the log, do you shout as loud as you can," said the Grouse.

The Turkey was so eager and excited that, when the Grouse gave the signal, he tried to shout, but could not raise his voice, and all he could say was, "Gobble! Gobble! Gobble!"

And since that day, whenever the Turkey hears a noise, he can only gobble.

When you arise in the morning, give thanks for the morning light, give thanks for your food and the joy of living. If you see no reason for giving thanks, the fault lies in yourself. ~Tecumseh

THE ELEPHANT AND HIS MOTHER, A Buddhist Thanksgiving Story

Long ago, in the hills of the Himalayas near a lotus pool, there was born a baby elephant. He was a magnificent elephant, pure white with feet and face the color of coral. His trunk gleamed like a silver rope and his ivory tusks curled up in a long arc.

He followed his mother everywhere. She plucked the tenderest leaves and sweetest mangoes from the tall trees and gave them to him. "First you, then me," she said. She bathed him in the cool lotus pool among the fragrant flowers. Drawing the sparkling water up in her trunk, she sprayed him over the top of his head and back until he shone. Then filling his trunk with water, he took careful aim and squirted a perfect geyser right between his mother's eyes. Without blinking, she squirted him back. And back and forth, they gleefully squirted and splashed each other. Splish! Splash! Then they rested in the soft muck with their trunks curled together. In the deep shadows of afternoon, the mother elephant rested in the shade of a rose-apple tree and watched her son romp and frolic with the other baby elephants.

The little elephant grew and grew until he was the tallest and strongest young bull in the herd. And while he grew taller and stronger, his mother grew older and older. Her tusks were yellow and broken and in time she became blind. The young elephant plucked the tenderest leaves and sweetest mangoes from the tall trees and gave them to his dear old blind mother. "First you, then me," he said.

He bathed her in the cool lotus pool among the fragrant flowers. Drawing the sparkling water up in his trunk, he sprayed her over the top of her head and back until she shone. Then they rested in the soft muck with their trunks curled together. In the deep shadows of afternoon, the young elephant guided his mother to the shade of a rose-apple tree. Then he went roaming with the other elephants.

One day a king was hunting and spied the beautiful white elephant. "What a splendid animal! I must have him to ride upon!" So the king captured the elephant and put him in the royal stable. He adorned him with silk and jewels and garlands of lotus flowers. He gave him sweet grass and juicy plums and filled his trough with pure water.

But the young elephant would not eat or drink. He wept and wept, growing thinner each day. "Noble elephant," said the king, "I adorn you with silk and

137

jewels. I give you the finest food and the purest water, yet you do not eat or drink. What will please you?"

The young elephant said, "Silk and jewels, food and drink do not make me happy. My blind old mother is alone in the forest with no one to care for her. Though I may die, I will take no food or water until I give some to her first."

The king said, "Never have I seen such kindness, not even among humans. It is not right to keep this young elephant in chains." Free, the young elephant raced through the hills looking for his mother.

He found her by the lotus pool. There she lay in the mud, too weak to move. With tears in his eyes, he filled his trunk with water and sprayed the top of her head and back until she shone. "Is it raining?" she asked. "Or has my son returned to me?"

"It is your very own son!" he cried. "The king has set me free!" As he washed her eyes, a miracle happened. Her sight returned.

"May the king rejoice today as I rejoice at seeing my son again!" she said.

The young elephant then plucked the tenderest leaves and sweetest mangoes from a tree and gave them to her. "First you, then me."

GIVING THANKS

AUNT SUSANNA'S THANKSGIVING DINNER, by Lucy Maud Montgomery

"Here's Aunt Susanna, girls," said Laura, who was sitting by the north window—nothing but north light does for Laura, who is the artist of our talented family.

Her words were a signal for Kate to hang up her violin and for me to push my pen and portfolio out of sight. Laura had hidden her brushes and water colors as she spoke.

Only Margaret continued to bend serenely over her Latin grammar. Aunt Susanna frowns on musical and literary and artistic ambitions but she accords a faint approval to Margaret's desire for an education. A college course, with a tangible diploma at the end, and a sensible pedagogic aspiration, is something Aunt Susanna can understand when she tries hard. But she cannot understand messing with paints, fiddling, or scribbling, and she has only unmeasured contempt for messers, fiddlers, and scribblers. Time was when we had paid no attention to Aunt Susanna's views on these points; but ever since she had, on one incautious day when she was in high good humor, dropped a pale, anemic little hint that she might send Margaret to college if she were a good girl, we had been bending all our energies towards securing Aunt Susanna's approval. It was not enough that Aunt Susanna should approve of Margaret; she must approve of the whole four of us or she would not help Margaret. That is Aunt Susanna's way. Margaret's chances looked a little foggy; but we hadn't quite given up hope. A very little thing might sway Aunt Susanna one way or the other, so that we walked very softly and tried to mingle serpents' wisdom and doves' harmlessness in practical portions.

When Aunt Susanna came in Laura was crocheting, Kate was sewing, and I was poring over a recipe book. That was not deception at all, since we did all these things frequently—much more frequently, in fact, than we painted or fiddled or wrote. But Aunt Susanna would never believe it. Nor did she believe it now.

She threw back her lovely new sealskin cape, looked around the sitting-room and then smiled—a truly Aunt Susannian smile.

"What a pity you forgot to wipe that smudge of paint off your nose, Laura," she said sarcastically. "You don't seem to get on very fast with your lace. How long is it since you began it? Over three months, isn't it?"

"This is the third piece of the same pattern I've done in three months, Aunt Susanna," said Laura. She did not tell Aunt Susanna that she sold her lace at the Women's Exchange in town and made enough to buy her new hats. She makes enough out of her water colors to dress herself.

Aunt Susanna took a second breath and started in again.

"I notice your violin hasn't quite as much dust on it as the rest of the things in this room, Kate. It's a pity you stopped playing just as I came in. I don't enjoy fiddling much but I'd prefer it to seeing anyone using a needle who isn't accustomed to it."

Kate is really a most dainty needlewoman and does all the fine sewing in our family. She colored and said nothing—that being the highest pitch of virtue to which our Katie, like myself, can attain.

"And there's Margaret ruining her eyes over books," went on Aunt Susanna severely. "Will you kindly tell me, Margaret Thorne, what good you ever expect Latin to do you?"

"Well, you see, Aunt Susanna," said Margaret gently,"I want to be a teacher if I can manage to get through, and I shall need Latin for that."

All the girls except me had now got their accustomed rap, but I knew better than to hope I should escape.

"So you're reading a recipe book, Agnes? Well, that's better than poring over a novel. I'm afraid you haven't been at it very long though. People generally don't read recipes upside down—and besides, you didn't quite cover up your portfolio. I see a corner of it sticking out. Was genius burning before I came in? It's too bad if I quenched the flame."

"A cookery book isn't such a novelty to me as you seem to think, Aunt Susanna," I said, as meekly as it was possible for me. "Why I'm a real good cook—'if I do say it as hadn't orter.'"

I am, too.

"Well, I'm glad to hear it," said Aunt Susanna skeptically, "because that has to do with my errand her today. I'm in a peck of troubles. Firstly, Miranda Mary's mother has had to go and get sick and Miranda Mary must go home to wait on her. Secondly, I've just had a telegram from my sister-in-law who has been ordered west for her health, and I'll have to leave on tonight's train to see her before she goes. I can't get back until the noon train Thursday, and that is Thanksgiving, and I've invited Mr. and Mrs. Gilbert to dinner that day. They'll come on the same train. I'm dreadfully worried. There doesn't seem to be anything I can do except get one of you girls to go up to the Pinery Thursday morning and cook the dinner for us. Do you think you can manage it?"

We all felt rather dismayed, and nobody volunteered with a rush. But as I had just boasted that I could cook it was plainly my duty to step into the breach, and I did it with fear and trembling.

"I'll go, Aunt Susanna," I said.

"And I'll help you," said Kate.

"Well, I suppose I'll have to try you," said Aunt Susanna with the air of a woman determined to make the best of a bad business. "Here is the key of the kitchen door. You'll find everything in the pantry, turkey and all. The mince pies are already made so you'll only have to warm them up. I want dinner sharp at twelve for the train is due at 11:50. Mr. and Mrs. Gilbert are very particular and I do hope you will have things right. Oh, if I could only be home myself! Why will people get sick at such inconvenient times?"

"Don't worry, Aunt Susanna," I said comfortingly. "Kate and I will have your Thanksgiving dinner ready for you in tiptop style."

"Well, I'm sure I hope so. Above all, don't let any of the McGinnises in. They'll be sure to be prowling around when I'm not home. Don't give that dog of theirs any scraps, either."

We promised to eschew the McGinnises and all their works, including the dog, and when Aunt Susanna had gone we looked at each other with mingled hope and fear.

"Girls, this is the chance of your lives," said Laura. "If you can only please Aunt Susanna with this dinner it will convince her that you are good cooks in spite of your nefarious bent for music and literature. I consider the illness of Miranda Mary's mother a Providential interposition—if she isn't too sick."

"It's all very well for you to be pleased, Lolla," I said dolefully. "But I don't feel jubilant over the prospect at all. Something will probably go wrong. And then there's our own nice little Thanksgiving celebration we've planned, and pinched and economized for weeks to provide. That is half spoiled now."

"Oh, what is that compared to Margaret's chance of going to college?" exclaimed Kate. "Cheer up, Aggie. You know we can cook. I feel that it is now or never with Aunt Susanna."

I cheered up accordingly. We are not given to pessimism, which is fortunate. Ever since father died four years ago we have struggled on here, content to give up a good deal just to keep our home and be together. We've been very happy as a rule. Aunt Susanna has a big house and lots of money but she isn't as happy as we are. She nags us a good deal—just as she used to nag father—but we don't mind it very much after all. Indeed, I sometimes suspect that we really like Aunt Susanna tremendously if she'd only leave us alone long enough to find it out.

Thursday morning was an ideal Thanksgiving morning—bright, crisp and sparkling. There had been a white frost in the night, and the orchard and the white birch wood behind it looked like fairyland. We were all up early. None of us had slept well, and both Kate and I had had the most fearful dreams of spoiling Aunt Susanna's Thanksgiving dinner.

"Never mind, dreams always go by contraries, you know," said Laura cheerfully. "You'd better go up to the Pinery early and get the fires on, for the house will be cold. Remember the McGinnises and the dog. Weigh the turkey so that you'll know exactly how long to cook it. Put the pies in the oven in time to get piping hot—lukewarm mince pies are an abomination. Be sure—"

142

"Laura, don't confuse us with any more cautions," I groaned, "or we shall get hopelessly fuddled. Come on, Kate, before she has time to."

It wasn't very far up to the Pinery—just ten minutes' walk, and such a delightful walk on that delightful morning. We went through the orchard and then through the white birch wood where the loveliness of the frosted boughs awed us. Beyond that there was a lane between ranks of young, balsamy, white-misted firs and then an open pasture field, sere and crispy. Just across it was the Pinery, a lovely old house with dormer windows in the roof, surrounded by pines that were dark and glorious against the silvery morning sky.

The McGinnis dog was sitting on the back-door steps when we arrived. He wagged his tail ingratiatingly, but we ruthlessly pushed him off, went in and shut the door in his face. All the little McGinnises were sitting in a row on their fence, and they whooped derisively. We rather like the urchins and we would probably have gone over to talk to them if we had not had the fear of Aunt Susanna before our eyes.

We kindled the fires, weighed the turkey, put it in the oven and prepared the vegetables. Then we set the dining-room table and decorated it with Aunt Susanna's potted ferns and dishes of lovely red apples. Everything went so smoothly that we soon forgot to be nervous. When the turkey was done, we took it out, set it on the back of the range to keep warm and put the mince pies in. The potatoes, cabbage and turnips were bubbling away cheerfully, and everything was going as merrily as a marriage bell. Then, all at once, things happened.

In an evil hour we went to the yard window and looked out. We saw a quiet scene. The McGinnis dog was still sitting on his haunches by the steps, just as he had been sitting all the morning. Down in the McGinnis yard everything wore an unusually peaceful aspect. Only one McGinnis was in sight—Tony, aged eight, who was perched up on the edge of the well box, swinging his legs and singing at the top of his melodious Irish voice. All at once, just as we were looking at him, Tony went over backward and apparently tumbled head foremost down his father's well.

Kate and I screamed simultaneously. We tore across the kitchen, flung open the door, plunged down over Aunt Susanna's yard, scrambled over the fence and flew to the well. Just as we reached it, Tony's red head appeared as he

climbed serenely out over the box. I don't know whether I felt more relieved or furious. He had merely fallen on the blank guard inside the box: and there are times when I am tempted to think he fell on purpose because he saw Kate and me looking out at the window. At least he didn't seem at all frightened, and grinned most impishly at us.

Kate and I turned on our heels and marched back in as dignified a manner as was possible under the circumstances. Half way up Aunt Susanna's yard we forgot dignity and broke into a run. We had left the door open and the McGinnis dog had disappeared.

Never shall I forget the sight we saw or the smell we smelled when we burst into that kitchen. There on the floor was the McGinnis dog and what was left of Aunt Susanna's Thanksgiving turkey. As for the smell, imagine a commingled odor of scorching turnips and burning mince pies, and you have it.

The dog fled out with a guilty yelp. I groaned and snatched the turnips off. Kate threw open the oven door and dragged out the pies. Pies and turnips were ruined as irretrievably as the turkey.

"Oh, what shall we do?" I cried miserably. I knew Margaret's chance of college was gone forever.

"Do!" Kate was superb. She didn't lose her wits for a second. "We'll go home and borrow the girls' dinner. Quick— there's just ten minutes before train time. Throw those pies and turnips into this basket—the turkey too—we'll carry them with us to hide them."

I might not be able to evolve an idea like that on the spur of the moment, but I can at least act up to it when it is presented. Without a moment's delay we shut the door and ran. As we went I saw the McGinnis dog licking his chops over in their yard. I have been ashamed ever since of my feelings toward that dog. They were murderous. Fortunately

144

I had no time to indulge them.

It is ten minutes' walk from the Pinery to our house, but you can run it in five. Kate and I burst into the kitchen just as Laura and Margaret were sitting down to dinner. We had neither time nor breath for explanations. Without a word I grasped the turkey platter and the turnip tureen. Kate caught one hot mince pie from the oven and whisked a cold one out of the pantry.

"We've—got—to have—them," was all she said.

I've always said that Laura and Magsie would rise to any occasion. They saw us carry their Thanksgiving dinner off under their very eyes and they never interfered by word or motion. They didn't even worry us with questions. They realized that something desperate had happened and that the emergency called for deeds not words.

We got back to the Pinery just as the train whistle blew. We had ten minutes to transfer turkey and turnips to Aunt Susanna's dishes, hide our own, air the kitchen, and get back our breath. We accomplished it. When Aunt Susanna and her guests came we were prepared for them: we were calm—outwardly— and the second mince pie was getting hot in the oven. It was ready by the time it was needed. Fortunately our turkey was the same size as Aunt Susanna's, and Laura had cooked a double supply of turnips, intending to warm them up the next day. Still, all things considered, Kate and I didn't enjoy that dinner much. We kept thinking of poor Laura and Magsie at home, dining off potatoes on Thanksgiving!

But at least Aunt Susanna was satisfied. When Kate and I were washing the dishes she came out quite beamingly.

"Well, my dears, I must admit that you made a very good job of the dinner, indeed. The turkey was done to perfection. As for the mince pies—well, of course Miranda Mary made them, but she must have had extra good luck with them, for they were excellent and heated to just the right degree. You didn't give anything to the McGinnis dog, I hope?"

"No, we didn't *give* him anything," said Kate.

Aunt Susanna did not notice the emphasis.

When we had finished the dishes we smuggled our platter and tureen out of the house and went home. Laura and Margaret were busy painting and studying and were just as sweet-tempered as if we hadn't robbed them of their dinner. But we had to tell them the whole story before we even took off our hats.

Aunt Susanna came down the next day and told Margaret that she would send her to college. Also she commissioned Laura to paint her a water-color for her dining-room and said she'd pay her five dollars for it.

Kate and I were rather left out in the cold in this distribution of favors, but when you come to reflect that Laura and Magsie had really cooked that dinner, it was only just. Anyway, Aunt Susanna has never since insinuated that we can't cook, and that is as much as we deserve.

GIVING THANKS

50 WAYS TO SAY "THANK YOU"

Albanian: faleminderit

Algerian: saha

Arabic: chokrane

Armenian: chnorakaloutioun

Bengali: dhanyabaad

Bosnian: hvala

Cherokee: wado

Comanche: ura

Croatian: hvala

Czech: děkuji / díky

Danish: tak

Finish: kiitos

French: merci

German: danke

Greek: ef-hah-ress-TOH

Hawaiian: mahalo

Hebrew: toda

Hindi: dhanyavad

Hmong: Ua tsaug rau koj

Icelandic takk

Indonesian: terima kasih

Irish Gaelic: go raibh maith agat

Italian: grazie

Japanese: arigatô

Korean: kam sah hamnida

Kurdish: spas

Macedonian: blagodaram

Malay: terima kasih

Norwegian: takk

Ojibwe: miigwetch

Persian: mochchakkeram

Polish: jenkoo-yen

Portugese: obrigado

Roman: Inajis tuke

Romanian: mulţumesc

Russian: spuh-SEE-buh

Samoan: faafetai lava

Saxon: bedankt

Slovak: dakujem

Slovenian: hvala

Somali: waad mahadsantahay

Spanish: gracias

Swahili: asante

Swedish: tack

Tahitian: mauruuru

Turkish: teşekkür ederim

Vietnamese: cho tôi biet

Welsh: diolch

Yiddish: a dank

Zulu: ngiyabonga

Doxology

Praise God from whom all blessings flow; praise him, all creatures here be - low; praise him a - bove, ye heav'n - ly host; praise Fa - ther, Son, and Ho - ly Ghost.

MUSIC

Music helps set the proper mood. This playlist, along with the sheet music on the previous and next few pages, will help inspire an attitude of gratitude.

93 Million Miles (Jason Mraz)
Autumn in New York (Billie Holidy)
Be Thankful (Natalie Cole)
Blessed (Martina McBride)
Count Your Blessings (Bing Crosby or Ali Matthews)
Everything Is Fine (Josh Turner)
Falling Leaves (John Denver)
Give Thanks and Praises (Bob Marley)
Holiday (the Kinks)
Homeward Bound/Home (mashup of Homeward Bound by Paul Simon and
        Home by Phillip Phillips, sung by the cast of *Glee*)
I Could Not Ask for More (Sara Evans)
I'm Alive (Kenny Chesney with Dave Matthews)
I've Got Plenty to Be Thankful For (Bing Crosby)
My Favorite Things (Julie Andrews)
My Thanksgiving Prayer (New World Waking)
Thank You* (Brianna Haynes)
Thank You* (Tori Amos)
Thank You for Being a Friend (James Taylor or Carol King)
Thank You Friends (Big Star)
Thank You Lord (Tamar Braxton)
Thankful* (Celine Dion)
Thankful* (Josh Groban)
Thankful* (Kelly Clarkson)
Thanking the Lord He Made You / Thanksgiving Prayer /
        I Thank You Medley (Johnny Cash)
Thanks a Million (Louis Armstrong)
Thanksgiving Song* (David Campbell)
Thanksgiving Song* (Mary Chapin Carpenter)
Thanksgiving Theme (Vince Guaraldi Trio)
This (Darius Rucker)
What a Wonderful World (Louis Armstrong)
*The repeating titles are different songs by different artists that happen to have the same title.

Jingle, Bells

J. P.   J. PIERPONT

Quickly

1. — Dash-ing thro' the snow   In a one horse o-pen sleigh, —
2. A day or two a-go   I thought I'd take a ride, And
3. — Now the ground is white, —   Go it while you're young, —

O'er the fields we go,   — Laugh-ing all the way; —
soon Miss Fan-nie Bright   Was seat-ed by my side;   The
Take the girls to-night,   And sing this sleigh-ing song;   Just

Bells on bob-tail ring,   — Mak-ing spir-its bright,   What
horse was lean and lank,   Mis-for-tune seem'd his lot,   He
get a bob-tailed nag,   Two-for-ty for his speed,   Then

fun it is to ride and sing A sleigh-ing song to-night!
got in-to a drift-ed bank, And we, we got up-set.
hitch him to an o-pen sleigh, And crack! you'll take the lead.

CHORUS (*Accompanied by jingling glasses*)

Jin-gle, bells! jin-gle, bells! Jin-gle all the way! Oh, what fun it is to ride

1. In a one-horse o-pen sleigh!
2. In a one-horse o-pen sleigh!

Simple Gifts

Lawrence Henry

'Tis the gift to be sim-ple, 'tis the gift to be free, 'Tis the
gift to come down where we ought to be, And when we find our-selves in the
place just right, 'Twill be in the val-ley of love and de-light.

When true sim-plic-i-ty is gain'd, to bow and to bend we will
not be a-sham'd, to turn, turn will be our de-light, 'Till by
turn - ing, turn - ing we come 'round right.

Sing and make music in your heart to the Lord, always giving thanks to God the Father for everything, in the name of our Lord Jesus Christ. ~Ephesians 5:19-20

151

THE LANDING OF THE PILGRIM FATHERS IN NEW ENGLAND,

A Hymn by Felicia Browne Hemans

Look now abroad! Another race has fill'd
Those populous borders wide the wood recedes,
And towns shoot up, and fertile realms are till'd;
The land is full of harvests and green meads.
~William Cullen Bryant

The breaking waves dash'd high
On a stern and rockbound coast,
And the woods against a stormy sky
Their giant branches toss'd.

And the heavy night hung dark
The hills and waters o'er,
When a band of exiles moor'd their bark
On the wild New England shore.

Not as the conqueror comes,
They, the true–hearted, came;
Not with the roll of the stirring drums,
And the trumpet that sings of fame;

Not as the flying come,
In silence and in fear;
They shook the depths of the desert gloom
With their hymns of lofty cheer.

Amidst the storm they sang,
And the stars heard and the sea;
And the sounding aisles of the dim woods rang
To the anthem of the free!

The ocean eagle soar'd
From his nest by the white wave's foam;
And the rocking pines of the forest roar'd,
This was their welcome home!

There were men with hoary hair
Amidst that pilgrim band;

GIVING THANKS

Why had they come to wither here,
Away from their childhood's land?

There was woman's fearless eye,
Lit by her deep love's truth;
There was manhood's brow serenely high,
And the fiery heart of youth.

What sought they thus afar?
Bright jewels of the mine?
The wealth of seas, the spoils of war?
They sought a faith's pure shrine!

Ay, call it holy ground,
The soil where first they trod.
They have left unstained, what there they found
Freedom to worship God.

Over The River And Through The Woods

Lydia Marie Child

Lively

Voice

O - ver the riv - er and through the wood, To Grand-fa-ther's house we go; the
O - ver the ri - ver, and through the wood - oh, how the wind does blow! It

Piano

f

horse knows the way to car - ry the sleigh through white and drift - ed snow
stings the toes and bites the nose as o - ver the ground we go.

O - ver the riv - er and through the wood, to Grand - fa - ther's house a - way! We
O - ver the ri - ver, and through the wood - and straight through the bar - nyard gate, We

would not stop for doll or top, for 'tis Thanks-giv - ing Day.
seem to go ex - treme - ly slow, it is so hard to wait!

Come, Ye Thankful People, Come

Henry Alford

George J. Elvey

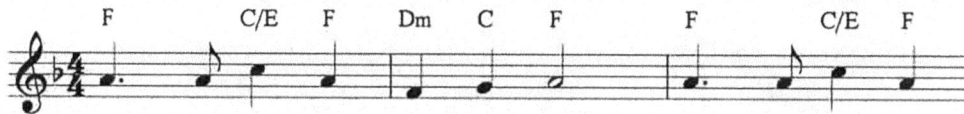

Come, ye thank - ful peop - ple, come, raise the song of
All the world is God's own field, fruit un - to His
For the Lord our God shall come, and shall take his
E - ven so, Lord, quick - ly come to Thy fi - nal

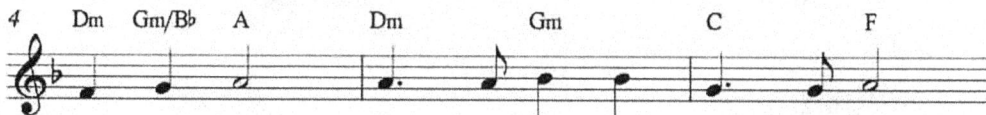

har - vest home: all is safe - ly gath - ered in,
praise to yield; wheat and tares to - geth - er sown,
har - vest home; from His field shall in that day
har - vest home; gath - er Thou Thy peo - ple in,

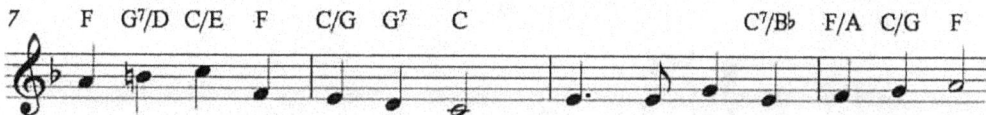

ere the win - ter storms be - gin; God, our Mak - er, doth pro - vide
un - to joy or sor - row grown: first the blade, and then the ear,
all of - fens - es purge a - way; give His an - gels charge at last
free from sor - row, free from sin; there, for - ev - er pu - ri - fied,

for our wants to be sup - plied; come to God's own
then the full corn shall ap - pear: Lord of har - vest,
in the fire the tares to cast, but the fruit - ful
in Thy pres - ence to a - bide; come, with all Thine

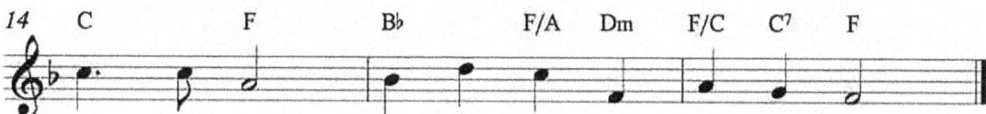

tem - ple, come, raise the song of har - vest home.
grant that we whole - some grain and pure may be.
ears to store in His gar - ner ev - er - more.
an - gels, come, raise the glo - rious har - vest home.

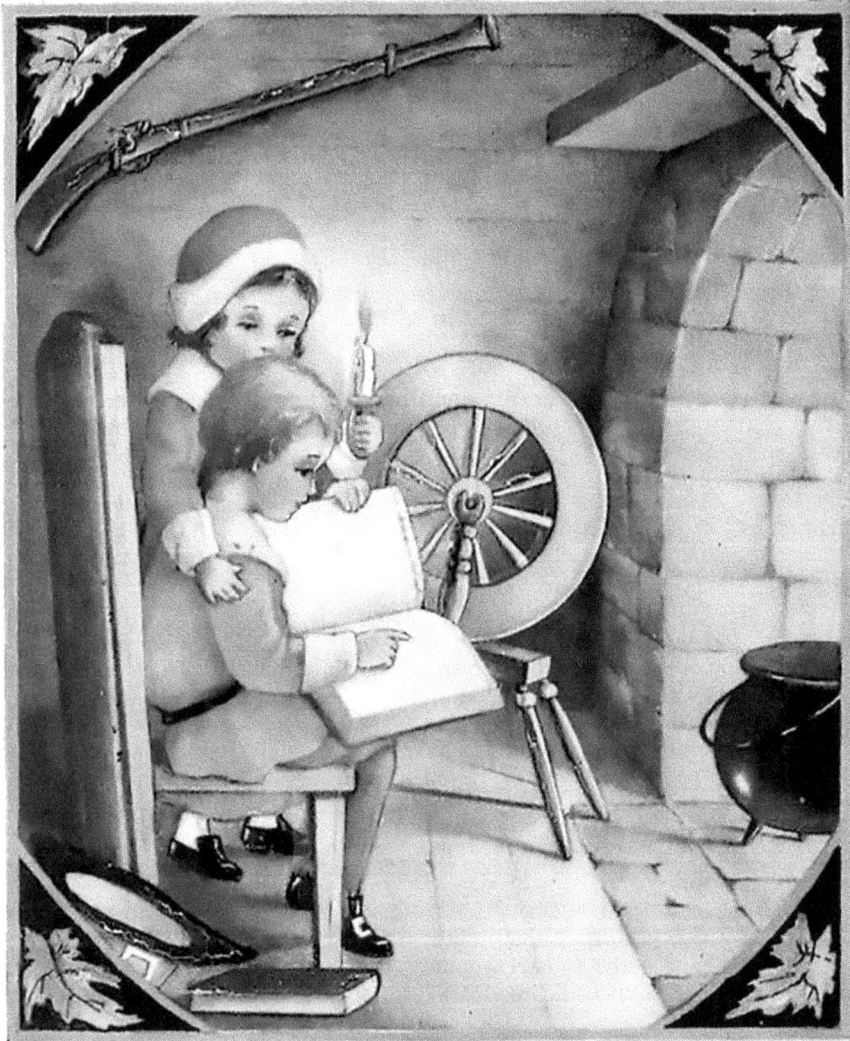

Let us come before Him with thanksgiving and extol Him with music and song. ~Psalm 95:2

Activities, Games, and Crafts

Thanksgiving is a time for togetherness, so try to arrange some time that everyone is not only sitting in the same room, but engaged with one another. Here are some ideas to help.

GROUP ACTIVITIES

To encourage interactions, try some of these group activities.

- Consider a tech fast. Even if everyone can't manage the entire day without their devices, at least have a set time – including the dinner, of course – that gadgets are turned off and conversations are with those present.

- Alternatively, use technology to connect with far-flung family. Set up a virtual conference (e.g., with Skype or Google Hangout) with those who can't be with you.

- Read a favorite poem or story related to Thanksgiving. Let someone who doesn't usually speak much choose it, and tell why they like it.

- Make a family cookbook. Everyone submits a favorite recipe, along with a memory related to the dish. It will be more special if they are handwritten. One person volunteers to make copies of them all and send a set to each family after the holiday. If this is done every year, soon you'll have a treasure of culinary family lore.

- If the weather is nice, take a walk after dinner to burn off some calories. If you live near a downtown, you can check out the display windows in the stores – and maybe get a Christmas gift idea or two as you observe what everyone is drawn to. If you don't live in town, take a country road and enjoy the fall colors.

- Spend an hour or two helping out at a soup kitchen. Few things make you more thankful than seeing how much more you have than the less fortunate. If you don't have that much time, make plates of dinner to take to a shut-in or someone who is alone for the holidays.

- Give thanks together by counting blessings. This can be done orally, with everyone telling something they are thankful for at the dinner table, or in writing.

- Each person can write their blessings on loose-leaf paper to be collected in a notebook, or on construction-paper leaves to be attached to a butcher-paper or stick tree. Someone should keep the notebook or leaves, and the next year they can be used to generate conversation and even more blessings.

- Or, have squares drawn on a large butcher paper like a quilt, and everyone décorates one square, incorporating something they are thankful for (either in words or art). It can be added to every year.

- A variation on blessing counting would be to give thanks for something about the person next to you, and go around the room.

- If people are not comfortable sharing publicly, have a blessing bowl, a large bowl into which everyone places a stone for a blessing, and can share with the group or keep private.

- Have a Talking Fork. After dinner anyone who used a fork has to share a blessing, memory, story, or anything they want. This is based on the Native American practice of speakers passing the pipe during council.

- Watch the Macy's Thanksgiving Day Parade together and see who can

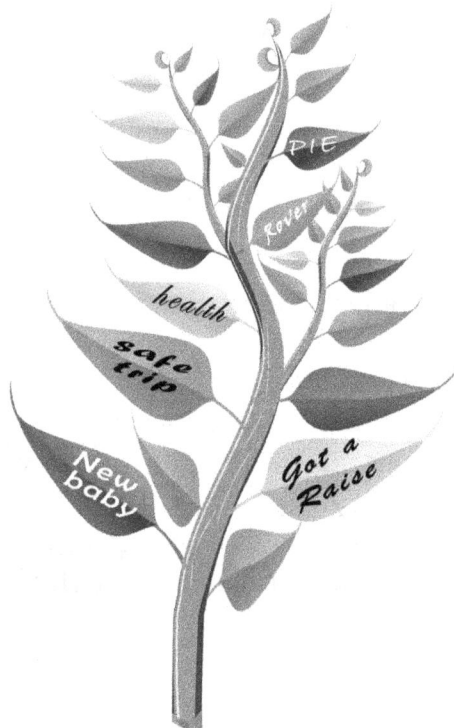

make the funniest jokes about the balloons.

- For a pretty thanksgiving ceremony, have a candle for each person. (Electric candles are fine; if using real candles, be sure small children are supervised.) One person lights their candle and names a blessing. They use their candle to light the candle of the person next to them, who names a blessing. Continue around the room until all have a lit candle. You could close this candlelight ceremony with a song of thanksgiving and a blessing.

- Look at photo albums together and share memories. This is a good way to involve younger people with the older ones.

- Play football. This is a tradition that goes back over a century and a half. In 1876, the first ever intercollegiate championship football game was held on Thanksgiving Day. The game between Yale and Princeton was a hit, and the tradition was born. Just a few years later, newspapers was commenting that the Thanksgiving Day Game was taking over the Thanksgiving Day Dinner, and by 1893 the *New York Herald* stated, "Thanksgiving Day is no longer a solemn festival to God for mercies given. . . . It is a holiday granted by the State and the Nation to see a game of football." It has remained a tradition ever since.

- Have board games, cards, puzzles, coloring books with pencils, dominoes, and other such activities for smaller groups to use when others are watching football or cooking the dinner.

- Have a pumpkin bowling tournament. Use mini pumpkins as bowling balls and plastic cups as the pins. Décorate the cups as pilgrim hats, turkeys, or other symbols of the season.

- Interview various people: the oldest person, the one who came from furthest away, the newest to join the family, or everyone. Ask questions about their life and things that are important to them. Write the answers down, and keep in book that gets added to each year. This is a wonderful way to get to know newer members of the family or people you don't get to see often. The book makes a wonderful keepsake as it grows. Hint: Don't ask yes/no questions. Ask what, when, how, who, where, why. Let conversations wander and unfold a bit, especially in a group – you never know what comment might spark a memory. When the discussion gets too far off, then bring it back.

- Catch leaves. This is harder than it sounds. There's an old Irish custom that every leaf you catch between Halloween and Christmas means a year of good luck.

- Act out a skit. It was popular in earlier days to have "home entertainments," which were skits or tableaus of historical events. *The American Girls Handy Book* of 1887 suggested for Thanksgiving the tableau "Landing of the Pilgrims: The good ship Mayflower has just touched Plymouth Rock. Pilgrim Father stands upon the rock, and reaches down to help Pilgrim Mother to land. The ship is a large wash-tub, which is placed in the center of the stage; its sail is a towel, fastened with pins to a stick, the stick being tied to a broom, as shown in illustration. It is held aloft by one of the children in the tub. Plymouth Rock is a table, occupying a position near the tub."

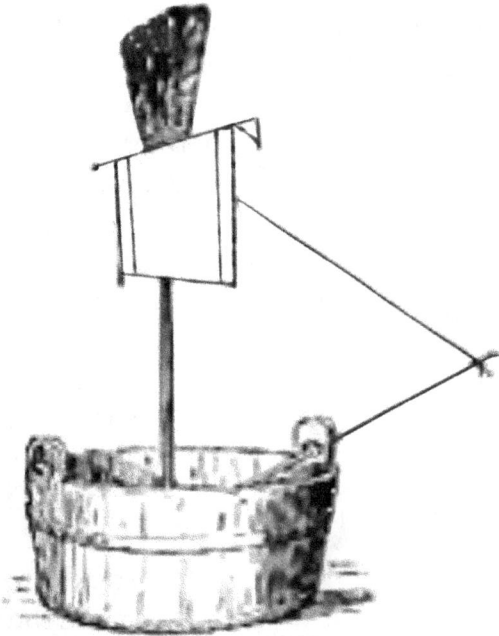

- Have a scavenger hunt.

- Play charades. An old twist: "Proverbs." In this Victorian parlor game, one of the players is sent out of the room and the others decide upon a well-known proverb which the absent player must, by asking questions, guess on his return. The answers to the questions must each contain one word of the proverb, in order as the words appear in the proverb. For example, if the players decide on the proverb "All is well that ends well," the first answer must contain the word "all," the second answer must contain the word "is," and so forth. If the questioner cannot discover the proverb, he must pay a forfeit. Examples of forfeits: imitate a donkey, impersonate a drunk choir director, or other nonsensical action.

- Although togetherness is important at Thanksgiving, find a few minutes of time alone to reflect on your most intimate blessings and meditate on the feeling of gratefulness they inspire.

No people on earth have more cause to be thankful than ours, and this is said reverently… with the gratitude to the Giver of good who has blessed us. ~Theodore Roosevelt

FOR YOUNG ONES, AND THE YOUNG AT HEART

These games are especially for the younger guests, although anyone may join in. The more the merrier!

- Ask the child who their hero is, and why. Then help them write a letter to their hero, thanking them for the actions the child appreciates.

- Go through the alphabet and try to name something to be thankful for that begins with each letter in turn.

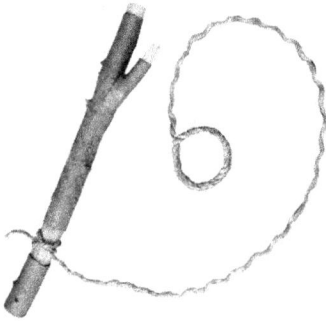

- Loop Stick: a traditional Native American game. Tie an 18" string or yarn onto the end of a wooden dowel or stick about a foot long for each player. Tie the free end of the string into a loop. The object of the game is to poke the end of the stick through the hoop, using only one hand. To make the game a little easier for younger kids, wrap the loop with masking tape so it's not as floppy.

- Turkey hop: Give each child a bandanna or scarf to tuck into their waistbands. Each player tries to steal everyone else's bandanna while keeping their own. For more hilarity, have them hop on one foot and flap one arm like a wing while playing. Anyone who falls or gets their bandanna taken is out; the last one in wins.

- Duck Catching. This is a Lakota game. Two people are the duck catchers. They make a bridge by clasping hands with their arms held high. Everyone else are the ducks. They walk in a circle around one duck catcher (thus going under the bridge) while chanting the sounds below. On the last measure of the song, the duck catchers drop their arms and catch the duck between them. The caught duck takes the place of one of the catchers, and another round begins.
Chant: Wee hee nah, wee hee nah hee nah, wee hee nah, hee nah wee hee nah, wee hee nah hee nah, wee hee nah, hee nah hey HO!
(Note: The lyrics are vocables, vocal sounds without specific meanings.)

- Popcorn toss: Divide players into pairs, each pair with a cup or small bowl of popcorn. One person tosses kernels one by one to the other who must catch it by mouth. One pair goes at a time, or at least have people supervising to count the kernels caught. The pair who catches the most kernels wins.

- Turkey hunt: played like Marco Polo but the person who is 'It' calls "Turkey!" and the others respond, "Gobble!"

- Peach-stone game. This was an Iroquois game traditionally played on the final day of the Harvest festival. The game was played using a wooden bowl about one foot in diameter and six peach-stones (pits) ground to oval shape and burned black on one side. A "bank" of beans, usually 100, was used to keep score and the winner was the side who won them all. Two players sat on a blanket-covered platform raised a few feet off the floor. To play, the peach stones were put into the bowl and shaken. Winning combinations were five or six of either color showing. The starting player shook the bowl; if he shook a five the other player paid him one bean; if a six, he was paid five beans. In either of those cases, he got to shake again. If he shook anything else, the turn passed to his opponent.

WHAT IF YOU'RE ALL ALONE ON THANKSGIVING DAY?

Every Thanksgiving is different, and some years may not bring a family gathering. When that happens, the holiday may be a source of loneliness, a reminder of lost or distant loved ones, and a time of depression. It is easy to say to count your blessings, but sometimes we all have trouble finding the blessings in our sadness. There is no easy answer or cure for such feelings, but there are some things that may help mitigate them.

- If you have family or friends to whom you can reach out, do so. This could take place in any of several ways. It may be possible to physically go visit them. Good friends will be happy to be available for you when you need it, even if they are busy. Take advantage of the opportunity if it arises.

- If that's not possible, perhaps a phone call would help you connect. Or, try writing a letter. This could be to a loved one who is not with you, or to someone who has made a difference in your life. Thank them for what they've contributed to your life, and tell them what they mean to you. Remember good times you had together.

- You don't have to know someone to reach out to them. Spend the day helping at a soup kitchen, or visit a hospital or elder-care facility and visit with other people who are alone. You may find that helping others brings you joy; and you may even find a new friend.

- If you know ahead of time that you will be alone, plan to help an animal shelter or similar facility. Usually, this must be arranged ahead of time, but the facilities are often happy for the help. Many times, their workers are out of town or taking the day off, but the animals still need to be fed and cared for. Or, perhaps a neighbor needs someone to look after their pet while they go out of town. In addition to helping the animals, you could be helping yourself: research has shown that interacting with animals brings contentment.

- Keep the lights on. Many people don't turn on lights for just themselves, but that could be a mistake. Doctors now know that darkness can sometimes deepen depression. Keep the environment bright, and it may help keep your spirits bright as well.

- Music also affects our moods. Play something that brings good memories. But avoid alcohol – it's a depressant.

- Above all, if you are concerned that you may hurt yourself, seek help immediately by calling a helpline or going to a medical clinic. There are people trained to help, but you won't know the difference they can make until you give them a chance.

ACTIVITIES

TRADITIONS FROM AROUND THE WORLD

Puritans and Native Americans weren't the only ones who celebrated the harvest, and modern Americans aren't the only ones who have a day of thanksgiving. On the contrary, such an annual event is common in almost all cultures the world over. Most of them are holdovers of rituals dating back to man's earliest days on earth. Some can also be traced to a specific incident in more modern times when a group of people gave thanks for a particular situation, like Canada's Thanksgiving, which dates to 1578 when explorer Martin Frosbisher gave thanks for safe arrival in Newfoundland by celebrating with a small feast.

The themes and activities are similar: giving praise and thanks for the harvest and other blessings of the past year by gathering together and praying, feasting, and celebrating. Despite that, there are some unique aspects to each. You may wish to incorporate some of these traditions into your celebration for a unique touch, especially if your family shares the cultural heritage.

The harvest festival of the Chinese is called Chung Ch'ui, held on the full moon of the harvest season. Lore says the moon is at its brightest and roundest on this day. The full roundness symbolizes completeness and unity, so this is a prime time for expressing love to your sweetheart in the moonlight. Family and friends communicate affection by exchanging mooncakes in pretty tin boxes. Mooncakes are round, yellow, palm-sized cakes of flaky pastry stuffed with a sweet filling. The cake is baked in a mold that leaves symbols of blessings (such as "peace" or "prosperity") on top. An egg yolk may be placed in the center, representing the moon. There is a legend that secret messages were hidden in mooncakes during wartime.

Tamil populations around the world celebrate Thai Pongal at the end of their harvest. This festival is a time to thank the sun and rain for a bountiful harvest. Neighbors gather to share their crops and give thanks to everyone who contributed to a successful harvest. Even farm animals are honored for their work in harvesting, with décorations, parades, and special snacks.

The word pongal means "to boil over." During Thai Pongal, celebrants boil rice, milk, and sugar together in a new clay pot. When the porridge boils out of the pot, everyone shouts "Ponggalo Ponggal!" to usher in prosperity.

Jewish families celebrate harvest with a week-long festival called Sukkoth. The word sukkah means booth or hut, which recalls the makeshift shelters used by the Hebrews as they fled slavery in Egypt for the Promised Land.

During Sukkoth, families build small huts out of leafy branches and foliage. Inside the huts, they hang branches of palm, myrtle, and willow, as well as fruits and vegetables like citron, pomegranates, and corn. Evening meals are eaten in the sukkah at dusk, after prayers of thanksgiving. Some families sleep in the sukkah.

The Vietnamese celebrate the Mid-Autumn Festival. Their festivities focus on the children. It is said this holiday began as a way to spend time with the children, who had been neglected during the hard work of the harvest. Children were viewed as innocent and pure, and thus the closest earthly connection to the sacred.

Before the celebration begins, parents help children construct candle-lit lanterns, and these are paraded down the street before the first light of dawn on the morning of the holiday. At night, children participate in lion dances. Some children beat a rhythm on drums, while others maneuver paper mâché lions through the streets. They stop at each home and business and perform, for which they are paid a little money. If two groups of lion dancers encounter one another, they will each put on their best performance, trying to outdo the other. Those wishing to commemorate the day in a quieter manner traditionally spend the evening gazing at the moon, contemplating life.

Japan's Labor Thanksgiving Day was established in 1948 to recognize the newly-guaranteed rights of workers. Labor unions hold festivals designed to highlight peace, human rights, and the environment. People express gratitude to one another for the work they've done throughout the year, and for the fruits of those labors. For example, school children may present drawings or small gifts to the local police in appreciation for ensuring their safety. People also spend time reflecting on their lives, and whether the results of their pursuits are honorable.

In addition, celebrants reflect on all things that come from nature, and express appreciation for it. Homes are décorated with lemniscates: knots formed by interlocking infinity symbols, which represent the interaction between humans, nature, and the cosmos. Cookies shaped like these knots are a popular treat during the holiday.

Although this is a modern holiday, it has ancient roots. Today's Labor Thanksgiving Day is held on the same day as the traditional harvest ceremony called Niiname-sai, which means "tasting of the first rice." The ceremony had the dual purpose of praising the hard work that produced rice, and expressing gratitude for the harvest.

The emperor would shut himself in seclusion and spend the night cleansing and purifying himself. In the morning, he would put on a ceremonial robe, and present an offering of newly-harvested rice to kami, the life-force of nature, in a special bowl of woven beech leaves. He would then partake of some of the new rice himself, along with some sake. Today, Niiname-sai is celebrated privately by the Imperial Family, while Labor Thanksgiving is the publicly-celebrated national holiday.

The Yam Festival is a celebration of the harvest in Ghana and Nigeria. Also called Homowo, which means "hoot at hunger," the festival is a reminder of a famine which the people overcame with determination and the hard work of cultivation.

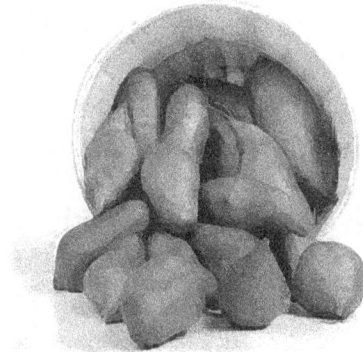

167

Throughout the harvest, the women set aside and save back the best yams for the festival. On the day of the festival, one boy is chosen to carry the saved yams through the village, with the rest of the children following. A chief blesses the yams, and then the people say prayers of gratitude. The yams are prepared, along with other foods, for a community feast. Before partaking of the meal, some of the food is sacrificed to the ancestors. After the banquet, people celebrate with drumming, singing, dancing, and sports.

Deutsches Erntedankfest

The Erntedankfest (harvest thanks festival) is celebrated in Germany and Austria in the fall, although each region sets its own date. This festival, like the American Thanksgiving, has both religious and secular components.

The day usually begins with a special church service to thank God for the gifts of harvest. The churches are decorated with artfully-arranged displays of the harvest before the altar. There is a sermon of gratitude and choral singing.

Afterward, there will be a parade of farmers and their families wearing traditional garb. Some ride décorated tractors; others carry farming tools or samples of the harvest. At the end of the parade, one woman is chosen as harvest queen, and presented with a harvest crown.

Other county fair-style entertainments follow. One popular event is the schürreskarrenrennen, or wheelbarrow race. The participants must wear full, traditional attire, including clogs. Music is usually a large part of the day. Bands play and various dances are held, including a blotschenball, or clogs ball.

In the evening, there is another church service at which the giving of thanks is again emphasized. This is followed by a lantern parade for the children, which culminates with fireworks.

ACTIVITIES

The Harvest Thanksgiving of the United Kingdom does not have an official date, but it is traditionally held on the Sunday of the harvest moon that occurs closest to the autumnal equinox. The festival dates to pre-Christian times when the Saxons offered the first ears of corn to fertility gods. When the harvest was completed, communities gathered for a harvest supper.

Many traditions of that festival have remained, and today Harvest Thanksgiving is marked in churches and schools with prayer and song. Homes and shops are décorated with baskets of food and fruit to celebrate a successful harvest and to give thanks. Food drives are often held, with the collection given to local charities which help those in need.

In recent years, the National Harvest Service has worked with schools to instruct children on the importance of agriculture. Students research local crops, plant seeds, and care for gardens. They harvest the crop and create harvest boxes for local elder-care facilities and homeless shelters.

Korea's harvest celebration, Chu-Seok ("fall evening"), is a three-day festival. Emphasis is given to family, both living and deceased. If at all possible, people travel to their birth home for the occasion.

The ceremony begins with an evening memorial service at the graves of the ancestors. Traditional dress is customary. The ancestors are remembered with words of praise and thankfulness, and gifts of food.

A generous full moon welcome for Chuseok

Thanksgiving Day is a jewel, to set in the hearts of honest men; but be careful that you do not take the day, and leave out the gratitude. ~E.P. Powell

Under the full moon, women and girls wearing traditional dress do a circle dance, called ganggangsuwollae, hoping to please the spirits of their ancestors. This dance has been performed for thousands of years, back to a time when people believed the sun and moon controlled the universe and women danced under a full moon to bring a good harvest.

Legend says that during the Japanese invasion of the 16th century, the Admiral of the Korean army ordered the women to dress in military uniform and perform the dance, confusing the Japanese and tricking them into believing the Korean army was much larger than it was.

After honoring the ancestors with praise, food, and dance, celebrants may partake of the harvest feast. Songpyon, rice cakes filled with nuts, seeds, and honey, are the main traditional dish. The cakes are steamed and served on a bed of rice. The celebration continues for two more days with games, song, dance, and wrestling.

America's Thanksgiving Day is also observed with a ceremony in the Netherlands. Many of the Puritans had lived in Leiden for several years before migrating to America. Pieterskerk (St. Peter's Church) contains many records of Puritans' births, marriages, and deaths. In honor of this connection, each Thanksgiving the church holds a special service to commemorate the hospitality the Puritans received in Leiden.

Day of Mourning, Day of Joy

When I was a child in school, each November was spent learning about "the first Thanksgiving." The "Pilgrims" (Puritans) were glorified as the first settlers of a wild land, as godly people who treated the native population fairly and only fought back when first attacked. The "Indians" were portrayed as "noble savages" who were helpful but uncivilized, and who needed the moral guidance and social refinement of white men to become better individuals.

The Harvest Feast

Of course, the Puritans were far from the first settlers: the indigenous population had been dwelling and prospering in the Americas for many centuries. Even other Europeans had been coming to the New World for a few hundred years. And while the Puritans certainly believed in God and tried to live as they believed He wanted them to, their actions in stealing food and land from the native peoples, and murdering them when they objected, is not a moral ideal.

171

Less than 5% of the U.S. population has native blood, so perhaps it's not surprising that the national narrative tends to ignore the perspective of Native Americans; but since the very survival of the European settlers was made possible by them, we owe it to Native Americans to consider their side of history's story.

In 1970, one of the few remaining members of the Wampanoag, Wamsutta Frank James, was invited to participate at an official Massachusetts state dinner celebrating the 350th anniversary of the Mayflower landing. He accepted, and prepared a speech. When officials previewed the speech, they felt it was not appropriate, saying, "...the theme of the anniversary celebration is brotherhood and anything inflammatory would have been out of place." Instead, they gave him some prepared remarks to make. He declined, and made his original version public. It read in part:

> It is with mixed emotion that I stand here to share my thoughts. This is a time of celebration for you - celebrating an anniversary of a beginning for the white man in America. A time of looking back, of reflection. It is with a heavy heart that I look back upon what happened to my People. Even before the Pilgrims landed it was common practice for explorers to capture Indians, take them to Europe and sell them as slaves for 220 shillings apiece. The Pilgrims had hardly explored the shores of Cape Cod for four days before they had robbed the graves of my ancestors and stolen their corn and beans. *Mourt's Relation* describes a searching party of sixteen men. *Mourt* goes on to say that this party took as much of the Indians' winter provisions as they were able to carry. Massasoit, the great Sachem of the Wampanoag, knew these facts, yet he and his People welcomed and befriended the settlers of the Plymouth Plantation. Perhaps he did this because his Tribe had been depleted by an epidemic. Or his knowledge of the harsh oncoming winter was the reason for his peaceful acceptance of these acts. This action by Massasoit was perhaps our biggest mistake. We, the Wampanoag, welcomed you, the white man, with open arms, little knowing that it was the beginning of the end; that before 50 years were to pass, the Wampanoag would no longer be a free people.

The tentative peace and cooperation of the 1621 harvest celebration can be appreciated by everyone; what is often forgotten is that it was followed by centuries of war, land theft, slavery, and genocide—almost always initiated by the white settlers. This cannot be a cause for celebration among those whose peoples were the victims of these atrocities, nor should it be for anyone. In view of the tragic outcome for their people, some Native Americans have declared the fourth Thursday of November to be a National Day of Mourning, a day to stand up and ask to be heard as they speak of the atrocities done to their people, and how it has repercussions to this day in the discrimination Native Americans still face.

Yet, even among native peoples, there are differing viewpoints. The anti-holiday sentiment expressed above is one of these. Another is that although the traditional view of Thanksgiving does ignore and misrepresent some important history, it also shows that it is possible for different cultures to come together in goodwill. Some feel a sense of pride for the generosity of spirit exhibited by their ancestors, and wish to focus on the example set at the "First Thanksgiving" of the cooperation between the two parties.

My family recognizes the dilemma, and we try to use it as a teaching opportunity. We have so much to be thankful for, and denying that doesn't help anyone. Celebrating the harmony and generosity of the First Thanksgiving does not mean we must forget the rest of history; extolling our own blessings does not mean we must deny those of others. We can affirm the guilt of the white settlers' centuries of brutalities toward the Native Americans and work to right them, while also rejoicing in our many blessings. We can learn from the past and be thankful that we are, however slowly, moving toward a future of brotherhood among all peoples.

Thanksgiving is time to celebrate and delight in family and friends, prosperity and gifts. It is a time to remember all we've been given, and share it with others. As you count your blessings, may you find true Thanksgiving joy.

Wishing you a cornucopia

full of blessings and Thanksgiving Joy

Resources

Below are resources for more information and further fun on Thanksgiving.

ORGANIZATIONS:

Plimoth Plantation
137 Warren Ave
Plymouth MA 02360
www.plimoth.org

United American Indians of New England
www.uaine.org

BOOKS:

Agel, Jerome. *The Thanksgiving Book*. Dell, 1987.

Baker, James W and Peter J Gomes. *Thanksgiving: The Biography of an American Holiday*. New Hampshire: University Press of New England, 2009.

Bradford, William. *Of Plimoth Plantation*. Boston, 1854.

Bruchac, Joseph and Murv Jacob. *The Circle of Thanks: Native American Poems and Songs of Thanksgiving*. Troll Communications, 2003.

Cheney, Glenn Alan. *Thanksgiving: The Pilgrims' First Year in America*.

Hanover: New London Librarium, 2007.

Curtin, Kathleen, Sandra L Oliver, and The Plimoth Plantation. *Giving Thanks: Thanksgiving Recipes and History, from Pilgrims to Pumpkin Pie.* Clarkson Potter, 2005.

Dexter, Henry Martyn, *1821-1890, Edward Winslow, and William Bradford. Mourt's Relation Or Journal of the Plantation At Plymouth.* Boston: J. K. Wiggin, 1865.

Drake, James D. *King Philip's War: Civil War in New England, 1675-1676.* University of Massachusetts Press, 2000.

Dunbar-Ortiz, Roxanne. *An Indigenous Peoples' History of the United States.* Massachusetts: Beacon Press, 2014.

Faust, Jessica and Jacky Sach. *The Book of Thanksgiving: Stories, Poems, and Recipes for Sharing one of America's Greatest Holidays.* Citadel Press, 2002.

Franzwa, Carrie. *The American Patriot's Treasury of Historical Thanksgiving Dinner Ideas: Old World Table Settings, Recipes, Games, Hand Crafts, and Party Ideas for Cultural Enrichment and Pleasure.* Oregon: TIPS of Oregon, 2008.

Gehring, Charles T., Ed. *Council Minutes, 1652-1654.* New York Historical Manuscripts Series. Baltimore, 1983.

Gorges, Sir Ferdinando. *A Brief Relation of the Discovery and Plantation of New England.* London, 1622.

Gragg, Rod. *The Pilgrim Chronicles: An Eyewitness History of the Pilgrims and the Founding of Plymouth Colony.* Washington, D.C.: Regnery History, 2014.

RESOURCES

Hillstrom, Laurie C. *The Thanksgiving Book: A Companion to the Holiday Covering Its History, Lore, Traditions, Foods, and Symbols, Including Primary Sources, Poems, Prayers, Songs, Hymns, and Recipes, Supplemented by a Chronology, Bibliography with Web Sites, and Index.* Omnigraphics, Inc., 2007.

Hodgson, Godfrey. *A Great and Godly Adventure.* New York: PublicAffairs, 2006.

Johnson, Caleb H., editor. *Of Plymouth Plantation: Along with the full text of the Pilgrims' journals for their first year at Plymouth.* Xlibris Corporation, 2006.

Kirkpatrick, Melanie. *Thanksgiving: The Holiday at the Heart of the American Experience.* New York: Encounter Books, 2016.

Koller, Jackie French. *Nickommoh!: A Thanksgiving Celebration.* StarWalk Kids Media, 2014.

Leach, Douglas Edward. *Flintlock and Tomahawk: New England in King Philip's War.* Vermont: Countryman Press, 2009.

Lepore, Jill. *The Name of War: King Philip's War and the Origins of American Identity.* New York: Vintage, 2009.

Loewen, James W. *Lies My Teacher Told Me: Everything Your American History Textbook Got Wrong.* New York: Touchstone, 2007.

Mann, Larry Spotted Crow. *The Mourning Road to Thanksgiving.* North Carolina: Word Branch Publishing. 2015.
(Note: *The Mourning Road to Thanksgiving* is a work of fiction, but has an informative Historical Background section and Preface.)

McKenzie, Robert Tracy. *The First Thanksgiving: What the Real Story Tells Us About Loving God and Learning from History.* Illinois: IVP Academic,

2013.

Paterson, Katherine, editor. *Giving Thanks: Poems, Prayers, and Praise Songs of Thanksgiving*. San Francisco: Handprint Books, 2013.

Philbrick, Nathaniel. *Mayflower: A Story of Courage, Community, and War*. London: Penguin, 2006.

Schultz, Eric B and Michael J Tougias. *King Philip's War: The History and Legacy of America's Forgotten Conflict*. Woodstock, VT: The Countryman Press, 1999.

Sifton, Sam. *Thanksgiving: How to Cook It Well*. New York: Random House, 2012.

Stratton, Eugene Aubrey. *Plymouth Colony: Its History & People, 1620-1691*. Ancestry Incorporated, 1986.

Winslow, Edward. *Good News from New England*. London, 1624.

WEBSITES:

http://www.powwows.com/2011/07/19/a-more-accurate-view-of-thanksgiving/

http://www.pilgrimhallmuseum.org/thanksgiving.htm

http://www.wampanoagtribe.net/Pages/index

http://www.educationworld.com/a_curr/The-Thanksgiving-Story-The-Pilgrims-Revisited.shtml

http://nmai.si.edu/sites/1/files/pdf/education/NMAI_Harvest_Study_Guide.pdf

http://www.thanksgiving-day.org/thanksgiving-around-world.html

Indexes

INDEX OF PRAYERS

INDEXES

INDEX OF PROCLAMATIONS AND HISTORICAL WRITINGS

INDEX OF POEMS

INDEX OF STORIES

INDEX OF MUSIC